ROADMAP

to

SUCCESS

Insight Publishing
Sevierville, TN

TABLE OF CONTENTS

A Message from the Publisher

I've done a lot of driving in my life and one thing I have been smart enough to have is a dependable road map. If you don't have a good plan to get from where you are to where you want to go, you will get lost.

I've known many people who have started out in business and thought they had a good plan, but did not achieve the success they wanted. A major problem for many of these people was that they had not sought good advice from people who had achieved success. If you don't learn from the experience of others, you might achieve success but you will probably get there the hard way. You might get lost down many side roads before you find the right one.

Roadmap to Success, is a mini-seminar on how to plan for your success. The successful people in this book have the experience that will help you find what you need to create your road map to success. These perceptive businesspeople were fascinating as they unfolded their own personal road maps and told me about their various success journeys.

I invite you to set aside some quiet time and learn from these exceptional authors. I assure you that your time won't be wasted. It's not often that you can access such a large quantity of quality information that will either get you started or help you get further along on your road to success. This book is an investment in your future—your successful future!

Interviews Conducted by:
David E. Wright, President
Insight Publishing & International Speakers Network

ROADMAP *to* SUCCESS

1

An interview with ...

DR. KEVIN FLEMING

David Wright (Wright)

Today we're talking with Dr. Kevin Fleming, a talented, one-of-a-kind mind that has combined two unique fields into one—neuroscience and executive development. After receiving his BA, MA, and PhD from the University of Notre Dame in Clinical Psychology, he quickly became tired of humanity's accepting response to psychotherapy's pseudo-success and put his brain power to consulting and coaching some of the world's top business and high performance clientele—a culture traditionally not tolerant to merely "feeling good." In this position, Dr. Fleming carved a niche "between the shrink and the coach" where his scientific knowledge about human nature and the strategies to work within the laws of reality that create nature meet. Such a perspective put him "beyond motivation" and mere self-help ideologies into hard core transformational work. Dr. Fleming's work speaks about barriers of leadership or behavior change not being an external issue predominantly, but one that is more of an internal addiction, fundamental to humanity; that is, to deny the reality and truth around us all and collude with the projections of the brain that so badly wants "to be right"—many times at all costs.

Dr. Fleming, welcome to *Roadmap to Success*.

Kevin Fleming (Fleming)

Thank you very much. It is a distinct pleasure and quite humbling to me to be included here with such top notch folks.

Wright

There are many bright and talented coaches and trainers out there with good intentions and ideas, attempting to clean up the streets of corporate America, whether it is in the areas of leadership, training and development, coaching, etc. What makes your work so unique and different?

Fleming

That's a good question. I'd love to think that my work's distinctiveness comes from the content camp, where what is offered from a guru is that sort of intellectual contribution about something that has never been heard or uttered before in a certain arena—that revolutionary kind of thing. This is what is most commonly thought of as the source of innovation, but actually, it is just one way of introducing substantive change or evolutions to a way of doing things. The other is in the profound linking and bridging of two (or more) prior established constructs, disciplines, or thinking camps to create something radically new and informative for a field—the whole is greater than the sum of its parts, kind of thing. To me, that is what I feel I am doing for the executive and personal development fields. I am instilling again a standard of intellectual clarity and richness around the power of integrating many important perspectives that influence us without our knowing and are typically not on an MBA program syllabus. These include such areas as cognitive neuroscience, futurism, behavior change science, addiction research, clinical psychology, and organizational systems thinking.

If the world is indeed dynamic and is changing so rapidly with competing, contrasting, and diverse information channels, it is an issue of prudence, in my opinion, to arm my clients with a Renaissance way of looking at problems. Multiplicity of perspective is not only the key to enhancing learning, nowadays, it is an issue of survival, given the increased complexity. There's a Darwinian intellectual "survival of the fittest" paradigm out there, and those ill-prepared to think systematically go extinct.

I feel I not only introduce this rich tapestry of ideas to a sometimes-myopic executive who tends to see reality one way (as we all tend to do), but in the process, through "collateral learning" or accidental learning, I show these individuals the stuff in between the content of things that actually drive change. What do I mean? Well, these are things that transcend information. These include: the unsaid value trade-offs underneath change, illusions inherent to "common" strategy decisions, viewing only first or second order implications of an action, ease of accepting half-truths around being "right," and the power of knowing knowledge in a more intelligent manner. Try to find a tips and tools success book teaching this meaty stuff that I like to call "practical complexity." I don't find it out there. What I do is strive to take this complexity and find a way to communicate it. Whether or not we deny the complexity of decision-making around us, reality doesn't care. It will win 100 percent of the time anyway—natural laws have a way of doing that to you.

Wright

So it sounds like "the way things are," be it reality, truth, or natural laws, is a big part of your message. Explain exactly what that entails when it comes to your thinking about executive development and attempts at being successful.

Fleming

Well, I think that's a very interesting question and one that is a lot more loaded than we think. You see, to me it is not about traditional models, tools, or practices being "wrong" or critiquing some solid approaches of the great executive development firms out there. Rather, it is more about an issue of incompleteness versus fullness of an approach. The logic here is that the philosophers taught us that many things that "make sense" are not necessarily and unconditionally true, despite passing that intuitive gut test we all have. And to make things more complex, some things that have passed the rigor of statistical testing don't have as much predictive validity as our gut.

So where does this leave us in this contextual quagmire? It leaves us approaching the tricky slope of human nature and executive behavior change with humility and a keen eye that is not easily fooled and if nothing else, purposefully seeks contrarian perspectives and discomfort, conquering pride within, to better approximate "truth"— what matters most, anyway.

You see, we were keen to know that IQ wasn't everything in predicting executive performance in the tests we created. Thanks to Daniel Goleman at Harvard, we now know more about emotional intelligence (EQ) as a better predictor of this thing we call "success." However, a couple problems potentially exist in the full unconditional acceptance of promoting EQ at all costs—and these cautionary statements say nothing about the merit of emotional intelligence in and of itself, may I add.

First, with the advent of multiple sources attempting to measure this construct amidst a market strewn with EQ-laden language everywhere, you now have bright and talented executives speaking the language of high EQ while masking more cleverly underlying character flaws. This is the danger of holding any "one" idea too close to the heart in an all or nothing way.

Also, regarding the IQ debate, the Flynn effect taught us all to be careful with assuming we had the end-all/be-all acknowledgment about the alleged racial issues with formal IQ testing. Though we did uncover the racial bias early on, we tended to ignore the generational increases of IQ on the white population, which were also paralleling the increases noted on the minority population when we attributed their success on the tests due to an increase in educational opportunities. Very interesting. It appeared that our brains were getting smarter over time. And it has been a relatively growing acknowledgment that the problem-solving aspects of the IQ test (versus other content or school educated elements like verbal aptitude or mathematics) could be getting a push from the media and informational technology. Technology and media have been forcing us to think more critically over time around solutions that used to be more 2-D and linear, and most IQ tests are not testing that stuff. Arguably, as Justin Menkes points out in his brilliant Executive Intelligence work, this critical thinking aspect is the mother ship for powerful executive success. Maybe it's not so much that IQ per se is not related to executive development, but that the parts we were traditionally measuring were not so pertinent. It is my prediction that a similar honing will happen with EQ over time and appropriately place emotional intelligence in a more fitting role in the whole picture. I believe there is an affective dimension to critical thinking that this IQ/EQ debate may be missing.

When one applies this different level of thinking to things we have traditionally accepted as linked to executive development, we come up with a "Fleming's list" of sometimes forgotten but radically important aspects of the truly successful individual. For instance, we talk a lot about accountability as crucial to executive decision-making, but I take this a notch deeper with my clients in their assessment; I look for their ability to discern between "decisions" and "choices."

Owning one's decision is actually half the battle if it comes from a more compulsive orientated, overly-rationalized, and a prior scripted part of our "habitual self." You see, our brains love automaticity. Patterns and accountability will always be colored by how one reached a decision that one has to be accountable for. Being accountable to an unconscious, non-free part of you is a "canceling out" element when it comes to the victorious picture of building the most aligned and healthy executive. Choices, in my opinion, are freedom-based and seem to come more from a right hemispheric-based "a-ha" light bulb, symbolizing the integration of heart and mind, and less from the dominant rational and logically sound place. I think we are creating more mechanistic versions of the successful executive by not further drilling down to such distinctions. If you think this stuff is nit-picky, I refer you to a great quote by Eduardo Punset that elucidates this issue quite well. He said something to the effect of, "Never before has it been more critical to discern between what is important and what is essential than in our modern times." Whether it is understanding the depth of the word accountability, applying wisdom, navigating masterfully through apparent paradox, or inviting an ultra-diverse team around you, getting executive development right (or rather "getting the thinking about executive development thinking right") has never carried such a price for missing essentials and concentrating just on "important stuff" as it does today.

Wright

You talk a lot about "brain-based understanding" regarding your approach with executives. Would you explain more about what that means and why it is so critical to personal and corporate success?

Fleming

Absolutely. We have a lot of people selling the "what you should do" type mantras to leaders and teams. Folks eat this stuff up mainly because: 1) it makes sense and there are no rational arguments against the things we are teaching, and 2) the mere acknowledgement of concepts leaves a lot of room for who is really accountable to implement and execute. This love of the "just right enough" superficial sounding stuff carries a higher cost when you spread this knowledge in a more diffuse way around complicated cultures and teams. Sure, from a neuronal perspective, exposure to new ideas will start the process of new brain connections, but we forget that integrating this good information into brains for long-term habit development takes repeated exposure and a committed system to support the new learning. Overall, the diverse nature of many of the things we train on leaves a lot of room for interpretation internally (in our brain) and externally (the corporate operations).

But even if we truly "get the message," practice it with good concentration, and take 100 percent of the message to heart, we risk not taking care of a critical aspect of the change process that our brains love that we forget. This includes the power of unlearning assumptions we hold precious, right, and true. Thinking about touching these sacred cows will naturally bring about anxiety within. Our brains want to maximize efficiency in this cost/benefit ratio comparison of doing something about the assumptions or not. Many times what is most efficient equals what conserves energy and that usually means protecting assumptions. This process, therefore, leaves us room to create more dissonant-reducing (versus consonant increasing) stories about why a certain problem happened in Company X or with Boss X. You see, our brains love to reduce anxiety more than it loves to see the fullness of things. This is something we have to strive to overcome, and the first step is to simply be aware of it.

But let me clarify this whole idea of combating the natural powers that be in the brain regarding this "unlearning" piece that I think is so critical. Though I do not believe we can unlearn hardwiring, we can re-learn and set up some competition of concepts (i.e., connections that are so ingrained one would call them part of our "identity"). I am saying something different than most people who comment on this topic and assume unlearning is not possible. What do I mean? Okay, we don't *literally* unlearn hardwiring. But we do unlearn our filters and biases inherent in all the cost/benefit ratios that come from comparing potential decisions that get beefed up with new information. So we do create new wiring with new experiences and competing values to impose value trade-offs that, when acted upon, effectively create an unlearning by virtue of ceasing a problematic behavior. It is in this sense that I am talking about initiating the power of unlearning on the human brain and making that more of a conscious process to clients who engage in coaching.

What makes this whole process hard, however, is the chemical rush we feel when we settle on a supposed truth about someone or something. One typically doesn't get an "adrenaline rush" for being appropriately self-critical, and as the great guru Joel Barker noted in his seminal book *Paradigms,* essential paradigm shifts to thinking and innovation also don't start with any physical sensations or stimulating cues. Usually, when we do become aware of it, it's too late. Consequences have cascaded.

To teach a leadership team about how a brain works actually gives an ROI unparalleled to most training efforts nowadays because the executives learn the counter-neuro forces within them that prevent learning—true transformative learning—from occurring. It is in this acknowledgment where they can truly begin to be successful because they learn the necessary pause and the required next step of inquiry, not action. Just like strategic planning means nothing if first, second, or third order implications to their ideals and decision-making aren't mapped out and intricately connected up first, brainstorming sessions end up being futile because the brain craves automatic patterns. Therefore, unbeknownst to you, this apparent "creative exercise" is a lot more predicted and rote than you might think.

Joel Barker's "Implications Wheel" is quite innovative and brain compatible because this tool puts forth an innovative technology "underneath the assumptions of our conversations" that can get at the unintended consequences of a strategy. Most of our training and coaching tools today don't do that. They share the same assumption—truth is in the word. Period. That sets up a conflict about which truth is better than which truth. Chasing this conflict rarely goes anywhere. Truth is Truth. Usually it is a both/and kind concept that has nuances. To understand it one needs the ability to see connections, links, and implicit trade-offs.

The brain needs to be taken into account whenever we assume we are being innovative and doing something different. Check and double-check. As Einstein said, no problem was ever solved on the same level of thinking it was created on. Our brains love to keep the assumptive processes on the same level. It requires therefore an extra paradigm-shifting push, more than the effort of our first hunch.

Wright

Okay, so I hear that we have to almost second-guess, in a healthy way, our thinking in the first place. Is this what you call metacognition? Tell us more about this.

Fleming

Yes, the word "metacognition" is a fancy term that comes out of the cognitive neuroscience literature. (I'm still struggling with a friendly way of phrasing that in the executive world because I know sometimes I lose people when I use it.) Metacognition is really just a fancy word that means thinking about our thinking versus doing multiple approaches or projects from assumptively the same base of thinking.

A metacognitive shift with a client occurs when all of a sudden the filter in the brain that is used to perceive the world lifts, and it's as if another lens is thrown in front of the person's eyes; his or her vision changes radically. This isn't just a minor shift either. Promoting metacognition can be very dramatic. Usually, when you're looking at problems of sustainability, problems of execution, and corporate transformation, your answers are going to typically lie on a deeper metacognitive level.

The problem is that in many cases, leadership teams do not want the problems that come with initial paradigm shifts (e.g., temporary drops in productivity, turnover, strategic realignments, etc.). In many cases, a have-your-cake-and-eat-it-too mentality prevents the process from even starting. We get too comfortable, reactively or fearfully holding on to what we have while ignoring the signs that it's time to change. We get the comfort of being right, while losing the fight that matters. The goal is to be effective and this will require change.

I had a CEO who missed his metacognitive moment when he chose another traditional corporate retreat planning session over a radical invitation to change assumptions. He ignored my recommendations when I told him that the internal dialogue of his team is compliant oriented and if he did another retreat his problem would be the satisfaction that he would feel. Somehow, he needed to get at what was not being said versus setting up methodologies that fed the verbal, linguistic side of things.

I also told him that if he didn't believe how common it is to feel that one is changing styles and strategies at a deep level when one is really not, I recommended that he have his executive team list some of the recent initiatives, policies, and change plans that he had rolled out and try to find a common denominator. Chances are they were different versions of the same assumptions previously made.

I told him it was time to make a meta-shift and to think about their thinking in many of the things that were believed to be valuable.

We all have information, thanks to Google. But few of us have knowledge, which to me is depth (versus breadth) and where mastery of illusions truly is conquered strategically. Said another way, the world may be flat in terms of information processing speed in the twenty-first century, but human beings mastering a concept and needing the ability to make their own connections themselves is a timeless law of humanity that is not affected by technology as much as we want so desperately to believe!

Wright

You have talked briefly about some of the deeper issues involved in the overhaul of the process around executive development. But assuming that the assessment process does indeed go to some of the deeper levels that you have described what exactly are you looking for in this A-level executive?

Fleming

Certainly, as I alluded to earlier, critical thinking is probably the mother trait of them all. As I mentioned earlier, Justin Menkes, in his book, *Executive Intelligence,* talks about this sort of thing and I am definitely a big fan of the argument he makes. I also think that the exceptional executive also has a very strong, conscious awareness of the different value trade-offs that are being made in certain moments.

Full spectrum leaders can see many perspectives simultaneously and can communicate masterfully to tiers of their companies' leaders who are seeing different pieces of the whole pie. This cognitive flexibility, nonjudgmental presence of the importance of all value levels, and unwavering commitment to communicate this importance with authentic engagement to the whole culture is a rare gem. I believe human beings are wired to be self-interested creatures that choose only to go above and beyond the "what's in it for me" impulse when they hold a value greater than that self-interest. If what I just said is true, then we are all in a precarious balance—at a tipping point—where self-centeredness/resentment/backsliding can get switched on in a heartbeat when we are offended or are not acknowledged. An executive who knows this *fragility* will be diligent and mindful and lead high performance as no other. And please note, being aware of humanity's fragility about this does not mean treating people with kid gloves. That phrase alludes to the way one is speaking not to the awareness itself. Be tough on committing one's self to looking for fundamentals of humanity; be compassionate in connecting attempts about it.

I also think an exceptional executive has conquered fear in his or her life. I think at the end of the day, fear fuels reactivity and reactivity fuels poor execution. I am also a big fan of looking all around the radar screen at all aspects of the executive's life because there are many parallels between family life and work life. A keen eye can discern some "natural" decision-making tendencies when the pressure is off and when one is presumably able to choose more naturally. In high stress corporate settings, this natural part of executives gets more opaque over time because they have learned the motions and the patterns needed but not necessarily desired.

I also think they've gotten a handle on what I call the half-truths of success, which is what my new book, *The Half-Truth High: Breaking the Illusions of The Most Powerful Drug in Life and Business,* is about. These are things that are very commonly accepted in the business coaching industry, but when taken out of context and misapplied poorly across time, they become linked to some subtle or extreme failures of thinking. I think they therefore understand half-truths of business life really well and are seeking, with ever more prudent perceptive abilities, a systems-wide answer to things. And this is not easy! I mean, we're learning more and more about how we miss things every day. In other words, we have two hundred billion bits of information coming at us in our brain, and we are processing maybe 5 percent of that at any moment. So what does that mean? It means that we're missing a lot of data as it comes into our brain. Well, exceptional executives are aware of this and are always seeking several opinions from extremely diverse individuals in addition to their own perception because they know that will approximate truth. I think that's a huge, huge trait.

The capacity to unlearn, as I noted earlier, is also big with executives' success— can they unlearn the things they've rationalized to be successful at a prior point in time?

Marshal Goldsmith, one of the eminent executive coaches of our day, has a great book called, *What Got You Here, Won't Get You There*. What he's implicitly saying is that a certain skill set needs to be unlearned and a more radically different set of skills learned when values and goals shift and as new problems get more complex. Great executives can make that train track switch very well. They can unlearn and learn again, so again, there's that flexibility piece.

I think what doesn't get a lot of press, but is pretty interesting as a predictor of success for executives, is the ability to seek and work well with paradox. The more I do this work, the more I realize that I'm more a philosopher than a psychologist, studying ancient laws of the "what is-ness" of things. I see paradoxes in things a lot more, and I think that not being uncomfortable with that is a very good trait and very predictive of great *true* success. This is really critical nowadays because I think the complex "order in chaos" type of universe we live in is not divorced from business. When we invite paradox, we engage with complexity and therefore reality. When one is aligned with reality, one realizes the craziness of this statement: in physics we have three laws that explain everything in the world and yet in management consulting it seems that we have ninety-nine laws that explain 3 percent of what really matters. This may be tongue-in-cheek, but you get the point. The exceptional executive is not what you build. It is what you get when one builds nothing but being at peace with "what is" in him or her and can work with others' "what is-ness" to allow the combination of free choice and a maximization of a vision to happen together. In this presence, the exceptional human being is what you *get* --not what you create through tests and numbers, pie charts and graphical recommendations. Much like the saying, "happiness is in the waiting room of happiness," I feel that the truly amazing human being is not something you go after to be. It is the byproduct of choosing well, accepting, and learning more about how to learn.

Wright

You certainly sound like a very different type of shrink. What are your thoughts of your other shrink brethren who have made the leap from the clinical world over to the organizational world as you have? Is this style or approach you are espousing common from your side of the clinical psychology fence?

Fleming

It's a good question. First off, I don't think that any psychologist who walks into his multivariate stats class in graduate school dressed like Elvis Presley singing a made-up song on his guitar titled "You Ain't Nothing But a Data Point, Not Fitting on the Line" is any sane human being (laughs). But I digress. Many called me the Patch Adams of my department because I had the courage to shake up things a bit and make us a bit less stiff and more "real." I sometimes think rule-breaking (with boundaries) is needed in the successful life. I didn't know it then but I think I still bring that "did he really say that?" effect into my conversations with leaders today.

But putting those memories aside, turning back to the original question, I guess I would first have to say that I would never come down on somebody who is entrepreneurial enough to leave something that may have some issue that doesn't fit with him or her, and explore something else. Especially with the rise of managed care, I see a lot of psychologists perceiving the squeeze fairly well in the clinical world, and seeing a lot of their autonomy and creativity that they needed to be an exceptional psychologist robbed by paperwork hours for managed care stuff. I certainly see a natural avenue here for a clinically-minded shrink (but not overly so). I mean, here we are as experts in human nature; we understand the brain and pathology better than anybody else, and we know how to set up relationships better then anyone else. So it does make sense from the expertise side of things.

The concern I have, however, is this: I get a lot of psychologists who want to be supervised or coached on how to be an executive coach or life coach. I usually have to be very careful about this because many of these people have motivations I question. Being unhappy with one thing and having a passionate call toward another can be two different motivational poles.

Marty Seligman, one of the greatest psychologists of our time and who is responsible for the Positive Psychology movement, really taught us that decreasing a negative or symptom in our life and increasing a positive or virtue in our life can be two different centers that aren't necessarily the same. If we confuse these internally, we will likely confuse them with our clients when they want to "change." One person's definition of change could just mean "stop doing something ineffective," and another's could be "stop doing something ineffective and play everything safe from now on." Yet another's could be "stop doing something ineffective and learn the most preferred skill in future instances." All these scenarios require artfully connecting with connotations of change.

I've got many clients who literally want to be only less depressed and still other people who say, "I'm less depressed, but there is something more to life then just making me less depressed, doc. Maybe I am missing something." Well, that's a whole other level of something to grapple with in a session. Or the parallel to leadership quagmires works here too; for some leaders it is really about transformational leadership—internally and externally—and for others it is leading enough to convince others that they are about change.

And so, I really think the critical issue here for psychologists who want to be coaches is: what is the true internal motivation and can you discern some of these finer points in your own life and with your own clients in clinical settings?

When I get phone calls from folks wanting to be coached, I look for a long train of decision-making to see the shrink world differently and start challenging it early on—a type of, "I-know-it-sounds-crazy-but-I-can't-help-but-see-things-this-way" kind of persistence of eccentric thought. To me, these types of psychologists, who have just enough rebel in them but who are also grounded in the principles and ethics of the field, are my ideal client to be coached. They can do nothing but offer a paradigm-shifting perspective to an otherwise unilateral, linear thinking base of business coaches. This is a burst of innovation that really matters and we need to innovate our thinking first, then our technology.

And to clarify, no, I am not an anti-shrink who feels there isn't a place for traditional psychotherapy. Certainly for many there is. My call for change within our field is more about what neuroscience is saying is a key component to accelerating learning and potential within, which is to constantly reinvent yourself for greater good (versus telling others why they are wrong, because this is not true change). According to neuroscientist Dr. Joe Dispenza, this is a key part of the profile of human beings who have transformed themselves. And to me, we cannot lead transformation if we are not doing this ourselves—with accountability for *not* doing it. Think of how many leaders who have others holding them accountable for not breaking through paradigms and challenging conventional thinking. Not many.

Wright

You have a distinct view of the corporate retreat phenomenon that's so common; would you tell our readers more about that?

Fleming

That's right, the thing about many corporate retreats is that they don't quite do what we think they are going to do, but they give us the perception and feeling that they will, which is actually a dangerous combination. It's one thing if a CEO could say, "Let's go do a corporate retreat that will actually do nothing to change things, but let's have a good time and make everyone feel as if we are, okay? Here we go!" That would be great to hear; at least we are aligned with reality. But since people learn a lot more on a collateral level (i.e., adventitiously or in-between-the-main-stuff-you-are-teaching kind of learning), one has to watch out what type of learning you are doing underneath your structured content. Implicit learning and assumptions are always found right next to an agenda or a meeting planner's prescribed sheet of events—they go hand-in-hand.

To promote a radical shift here, I've always thought what would be interesting is to prepare HR and OD staff for the presence of this phenomenon by "pulling them into what's really going on here" with a reality television show type of video of a corporate retreat. I guarantee it would make them think twice about budgeting for something like this next quarter. It would also jumpstart their creative heads and hearts to better align with "what is" in their company. What do I mean? In this show, corporate retreat participants would be filmed in and out of the event sessions having off-the-cuff and transparent dialogues about what they think of the speaker and topics. Coveted secrets would be "spilled" to certain divisional operations by way of confessional booths (video diaries) where folks tell it all about so and so. Talk about making a 360 degree assessment look stale! All and all, it would be a show about "the internal dialogue" of employees.

And if you think this is just more of a metaphoric play on a reality show to make a point here, think again. Steven Johnson, in his mind-bending book called *Everything Bad is Good For You,* talks about how pop culture television is not only "not disintegrating" our minds and brains, but actually making us smarter. He analyzes reality television shows and the mental modeling around the intense social networking that it teaches observers. One may think that television viewers are passively tuning out with the flat screen television; but rather, we are participating in critical thinking, such as what would we do in those double-blind scenarios of reality show relationships? Through neuroplasticity we are reshaping our brains to be better prepared for the real life cost/benefit ratios of trying to navigate truth in a half-truth social world where agendas rule. This kind of television program is actually enriching our prefrontal cortex because we are navigating this stuff every day anyway, even if we minus out the artificiality of certain settings.

If this is a true argument, it makes an important case to re-evaluate whether or not our corporate training methodologies used on these two-dimensional corporate retreat escapades really match the complex neural networking and mapping we are responding to every day back in the office. If not, maybe our corporate retreats, not pop culture media—the token fall guy—are making us dumber (if not, certainly ill-prepared for the non-rope course reality that we know).

Wright

You're recent book is titled, *The Half-Truth High: Breaking the Illusions of the Most Powerful Drug in Life and Business.* How did you come up with that title, and what exactly is the book about?

Fleming

The title has an interesting evolution that is not typical, I would imagine, of other business books. You see, I attended Notre Dame and, as a Catholic, was raised to love many of the great theologians of our day. My favorite was C. S. Lewis. While at the University, I was exposed to his classic, *The Screwtape Letters.* I fell in love with the brilliant methodology in this book. What C. S. Lewis did was create this dialogue, through the writing of letters, between a father demon of sorts and his nephew, Wormwood, about how to secure the damnation of earthly mankind. But what was really interesting about it was the insidious ways in which it was done. The plans made did not use the stereotypical means of evil such as brute force or overt destruction; but rather, predominantly through excessive confusion. They utilized things that weren't so bad on the surface but over time could erode and tie up neurotically the most noble soul. The way, therefore, to best prevent insight and truth was to make people think that they were on the right path, but in actuality they were far from the righteous path.

So that's where I came up with the idea over time (because I've reread this book over the years) that the most insidious thing we can do for change is to sell half-truths, not "not do" anything at all, which is what people want to think is the true nemesis to change. You know, we clearly can read and see things that are not good for us. If someone came up to a company leader and said, "I think you all need to have a notorious convicted murderer as your keynote speaker next week," I think we'd all agree that's probably not going to be good for the spirit and integrity of the company. But what's more difficult to discern are the half-truths of success because they wear no sign per se on their head, and instead, evoke a certain kind of reasonability among the people hearing the ideas.

Before we get into an example, let me tell you how the book was divided. I wanted to tap into three of the most vulnerable areas in modern society where using half-truths is at work. The book is made up of three sections: the half-truths of psychotherapy, the half-truths of business coaching, and the half-truths of the Judaeo-Christian culture. (The latter, as you know, is riddled with a lot of politics and contention these days amid the backdrop of Islam that has brought religion issues front and center more then ever.) In essence, I wanted to offer a section of the book that touched on some of the real-world issues out there now.

So let's look at one of the half-truths I note in the book: "Just do it." It sounds good and reasonable, right? It certainly makes sense for the victim, the lazy one, or for validation of all the enthusiastic passionate ones out there. However, if you dive into this thinking a bit deeper you can catch more subtly an implicit half-truth that needs "to be owned" and inquired about more delicately before such a mantra could graduate to the full truth dictionary of definitions, so to speak. What do I mean? The half-truth that I think is implicitly in there is this (as it speaks to us in a kind of Screwtape-type letter) all knowing instructional-like way:

> *Just do it—Search for most of the elements in your life where a just-do-it attitude has gotten the job done, and use that as your proof that you're getting things done in other realms of your life, when in reality, "just doing it" is actually missing the boat, including all the complexities, nuances, and the under-the-radar-screen stuff that you need to address. But when you feel a pang, continue to move on because the consistent action and commitment to moving will ensure you that you are not stuck.*

This sounds so reasonable, doesn't it? Don't you know a few people like this who plow through life, not with malice but with a self-justified logic like the above?

So you can see I am trying to get people to slow down a bit and inquire. I want them to wonder more completely about why they are doing what they are doing. I'm attempting to call their brain out on its "automatic sentence completion" tendencies. Instead, I want them to double-check and reread all the meta-level scripts that are being filed away about their thinking and why they are doing what they are doing. The best red marks from your meanest teacher on your homework papers could probably not catch the crafty half-truths that you have filed away as "gospel."

And yes, some people may say that I am suggesting we all become the neurotic Woody Allen character, but certainly that is not so. Neuroticism is excessive inquiry in a looping fashion that has no proven impact or value evidenced in behavior change. It's thinking the same uncritical way over and over while expecting change irrationally. I am talking about inquiry with intentionality and intelligence—changing assumptions and paradigms inside thoughts so as to make your goal of behavior change less insane and more of a reality.

Wright

You have mentioned a quote earlier on that I want to go back to. It was from Eduardo Punset about discerning between what is important and what is essential. I am seeing it in so much of what you are doing. What exactly does this mean?

Fleming

I fell in love with this quote when I read his book, *The Happiness Trip,* it was somewhere in there. I remember writing it down on a scrap of paper and thinking about it for many days. It hit me that its power is in the two poles it compares: importance and essence. When framed this way, it forced reason to be more precise and more reliable over time. It raised the bar of critical thinking. And I think that is what our culture is forcing us to do inside all our decisions these days. I think we may have the best technology for entertainment or brain soothing activities, but our thinking quality for social complexities pales in comparison. We have lost the art of thinking well. Even our rationalizations have evolved hand-in-hand with our higher IQs.

Case in point: In *Harvard Business Review's* February 2008 edition, a very interesting article was written called "How Honest People Cheat" by Dan Ariely. In this provocative piece, an enlightening notion about humanity was uncovered that I think shows the need to better measure such finer discernments of our thinking these days.

While most people would agree that our society is not predominantly made up of overt liars and over-the-top sociopaths. One would have to admit that many of us "stretch boundaries" and evoke our dishonest potential in more subtle ways. They are masked in the whole "how much can we get away without being caught" mindset. And so, in some university experiments that are set up to test under what conditions otherwise honest people would cheat, some interesting observations were made. First, when tempted, most of us are willing to be a "little dishonest" regardless of the risks. Secondly, even when we have no chance of getting caught, few of us really become wild liars to an extreme, and exploit the situation. It is as if our conscience puts some sort of limit on us. Lastly, it appears as if we fall victim to justifying our manipulations the further removed we are from cash or monetary stakes. That is, nonmonetary exchanges seem to give us more latitude for half-truths.

And given that life is made up mostly of these types of exchanges, I argue that Punset's quote is right on in telling us we must keep up with this closing gap between what we think is important (which could be a half-truth) and what is truly essential. This happens because there are more and more negative forces telling us they are essentials; but they aren't.

What are some of these things that I think are the essential things to know? Well, they may sound rather heady but these three principles, if you think about it, really do give you a brilliant framework to catch your half-truths:

First, I believe in the psychological law of reactivity. For every action there is an equal and opposite reaction. If you resist this, then the message to drop your foolishness will get stronger in terms of negative consequences and will typically lead you eventually to this point of reason. Many people try to fight nature and the law of gravity and they lose. But if you fight this, the dangerous part is not in your pain, it is in the attachment you feel to the thing you push against—you become the thing you push against. Any belief should be held up to the light for its beauty and truth to be fully seen. Said another way, seeing one's decision-making outside of an interconnected system of choices and consequences is a violation of what is-ness and eventually will show you the error of your ways, even if in some subtle manner. If you push down on an air bubble, it is going to come up somewhere.

Secondly, no two objects can occupy the same space at the same time. This physics notion sounds trivial, but is it? There are many professionals who, if you don't slow their angry diatribes down, violate reality as they try to mix two emotions, for instance, together at the same time and place. Since many decisions—good and bad—are born from the affective dimension, this essence principle becomes a good one to know and coach on.

I also try to take apart sentences when executives attempt to inadvertently trick me in the need for speed in what they are saying. Nine times out of ten there is some push to violate awareness of this law and blow off the table the actual trade-off that displaced one thing for another.

Third, if you let anything be as it is and complete its "cycle" of behavior, it will go to fruition and eventually disappear. Our fear and perceived double-binds make us think that something needs to be controlled or fixed when we will actually do more harm both to the actors themselves and to the "reap-and-sow" process that defines all that we do and "that is."

To me, these are the things of essence that ground us. They are certainly the common denominators of many perceived problems in attempts to be successful. Success is what happens when you align with natural laws. We have brainwashed ourselves that success is something you do to yourself in some prescribed code of things. Actually, the ignorance factor around us has grown so much that the contrast effect has led us to believe success is something we do to climb the ladder. But, nowadays, I think success is climbing back out of the hole we have created to the ground base of reality. If we can climb this ladder, it is the most essential thing we can do.

Wright

In a market saturated with success books, all promising a certain taste of it if you do xyz, what promises do you make, then, if a client chooses to work with you?

Fleming

I promise people that they will know the truth of how ready they *really* are to seek the things they say they want. In my years of doing this work, I have grown to become comfortably skeptical about the script of what people say they want to do in a change effort. Many times this is the "should" part of them speaking and it is difficult to discern, so I like to tilt the scale so dramatically that the compliant folks fall off—the angle is too tough for their weak heart and myopic eyes.

I promise folks that they will become more acutely aware of the trade-offs and implications of their supposed choices. This is a very personalized process and one that, if chosen, will always trump the compliant process that dutifully engages, but for inauthentic reasons.

And assuming one approaches the change process with commitment not compliance, I promise my clients that their change plans will be full of what Jim Collins called "catalytic mechanisms"—things that are truth detectors and air-tight governors on their decisions that prevent their failure. These are powerful and not for the weak-hearted.

Jim tells a story about a company searching for a catalytic mechanism to ensure their empty words about being committed to "customer service." The answer? Allow customers to cross out the amount on an invoice and write their own amount in and the reason why they are not paying full price. Amazing. But this is a true, air-tight process to ensure you are really doing what you say in your coaching that you want to do. This decision may not work for you and your company, but I say that the principle remains. Putting the same air-tight intensity around what you *say* matters to you and your team.

My clients are creatively challenged in the same way to ensure preventing the inadvertent building up of half-truths while spending money and time on illusions. I wrote an article recently for *Executive Decision* magazine titled "ROI: Return on Investment or Return on Illusion?" I discuss many of the metric issues that plague us in this search for air-tight truth and transparency in our efforts. It's a lot trickier then we think.

Lastly, I promise my clients that I am not God and cannot change the order of things—to give them no pain in the process of transformation. There is always the parenthetical portion to growth and development that is unsaid but there. For example, "Doc I want—(and please don't let it hurt too badly or take away another thing that I actually want more but won't tell you upfront)."

My clients get real with me right off the bat. It may not feel good, but it gets real. I have learned that if you seek reality it may not feel good, but you will find lasting joy. (And the good news is that there are collective parallels here, not just for individuals, but for teams and cultures) I don't know about you, but I will take that any day; it doesn't sound like a trade-off to me!

Wright

Well, what an interesting conversation. I have really learned a lot and I appreciate the time you've taken to answer all these questions this afternoon.

Fleming

It's my pleasure; it's really good to be with you.

Wright

Today we've been talking with Dr. Kevin Fleming, who has combined in a fascinating way neuroscience and executive development thinking that is bold and truth-based. Definitely what our world needs to today.

Dr. Fleming, thank you so much for being with us today on *Roadmap to Success.*

Fleming

My pleasure.

ABOUT DR. FLEMING

Dr. Fleming is President and CEO of an international executive development and personal coaching firm concentrating on aligning best practice ideas with neuroscience and brain excellence. He is trained in neuropsychology and is a life/executive coach that has been cited as an expert in The New York Times and Christian Science Monitor. His latest book, *The Half-Truth High*, prompted a request to speak to the Ministers and Prime Ministers of Jordan and United Arab Emirates. He is  an expert columnist on "Transformations" for Executive Decision magazine. Richard Koch, bestselling author of The 80-20 Principle has noted Dr. Fleming's work as "a wonderfully authentic approach from the shrink who doesn't like shrinks."

Dr. Kevin J. Fleming
P.O. Box 11840
Jackson Hole, WY 83002
888-833-4580
Kevin@effectiveexecutivecoaching.com
www.DrKevinFleming.com

ROADMAP to SUCCESS

2

An interview with...

DR. STEPHEN COVEY

David E. Wright (Wright)

We're talking today with Dr. Stephen R. Covey, cofounder and vice-chairman of Franklin Covey Company, the largest management company and leadership development organization in the world. Dr. Covey is perhaps best known as author of *The 7 Habits of Highly Effective People*, which is ranked as a number one best-seller by the New York Times, having sold more than fourteen million copies in thirty-eight languages throughout the world. Dr. Covey is an internationally respected leadership authority, family expert, teacher, and organizational consultant. He has made teaching principle-centered living and principle-centered leadership his life's work. Dr. Covey is the recipient of the Thomas More College Medallion for Continuing Service to Humanity and has been awarded four honorary doctorate degrees. Other awards given Dr. Covey include the Sikh's 1989 International Man of Peace award, the 1994 International Entrepreneur of the Year award, Inc. magazine's Services Entrepreneur of the Year award, and in 1996 the National Entrepreneur of the Year Lifetime Achievement award for Entrepreneurial leadership. He has also been recognized as one of Time magazine's twenty-five most influential Americans and one of Sales and Marketing Management's top twenty-five power brokers. As the father of nine and grandfather of forty-four, Dr. Covey received the 2003 National Fatherhood Award, which he says is the most meaningful award he has ever received. Dr. Covey earned his undergraduate degree from the University of Utah, his MBA from Harvard, and completed his doctorate at Brigham Young University. While at Brigham Young he served as assistant to the President and was also a professor of Business Management and Organizational Behavior.

Dr. Covey, welcome to *Roadmap to Success.*

Dr. Stephen Covey (Covey)

Thank you.

Wright

Dr. Covey, most companies make decisions and filter them down through their organization. You, however, state that no company can succeed until individuals within it succeed. Are the goals of the company the result of the combined goals of the individuals?

Covey

Absolutely—if people aren't on the same page, they're going to be pulling in different directions. To teach this concept, I frequently ask large audiences to close their eyes and point north, and then to keep pointing and open their eyes. They find themselves pointing all over the place. I say to them, "Tomorrow morning if you want a similar experience, ask the first ten people you meet in your organization what the purpose of your organization is and you'll find it's a very similar experience. They'll point all over the place." When people have a different sense of purpose and values, every decision that is made from then on is governed by those. There's no question that this is one of the fundamental causes of misalignment, low trust, interpersonal conflict, interdepartmental rivalry, people operating on personal agendas, and so forth.

Wright

Is that primarily a result of an inability to communicate from the top?

Covey

That's one aspect, but I think it's more fundamental. There's an inability to involve people—an unwillingness. Leaders may communicate what their mission and their strategy is, but that doesn't mean there's any emotional connection to it. Mission statements that are rushed and then announced are soon forgotten. They become nothing more than just a bunch of platitudes on the wall that mean essentially nothing and even create a source of cynicism and a sense of hypocrisy inside the culture of an organization.

Wright

How do companies ensure survival and prosperity in these tumultuous times of technological advances, mergers, downsizing, and change?

Covey

I think that it takes a lot of high trust in a culture that has something that doesn't change—principles—at its core. There are principles that people agree upon that are valued. It gives a sense of stability. Then you have the power to adapt and be flexible when you experience these kinds of disruptive new economic models or technologies that come in and sideswipe you. You don't know how to handle them unless you have something you can depend upon.

If people have not agreed to a common set of principles that guide them and a common purpose, then they get their security from the outside and they tend to freeze the structure, systems, and processes inside and they cease becoming adaptable. They don't change with the changing realities of the new marketplace out there and gradually they become obsolete.

Wright

I was interested in one portion of your book, The 7 Habits of Highly Effective People, where you talk about behaviors. How does an individual go about the process of replacing ineffective behaviors with effective ones?

Covey

I think that for most people it usually requires a crisis that humbles them to become aware of their ineffective behaviors. If there's not a crisis the tendency is to perpetuate those behaviors and not change.

You don't have to wait until the marketplace creates the crisis for you. Have everyone accountable on a 360-degree basis to everyone else they interact with—with feedback either formal or informal—where they are getting data as to what's happening. They will then start to realize that the consequences of their ineffective behavior require them to be humble enough to look at that behavior and to adopt new, more effective ways of doing things.

Sometimes people can be stirred up to this if you just appeal to their conscience—to their inward sense of what is right and wrong. A lot of people sometimes know inwardly they're doing wrong, but the culture doesn't necessarily discourage them from continuing that. They either need feedback from people or they need feedback from the marketplace or they need feedback from their conscience. Then they can begin to develop a step-by-step process of replacing old habits with new, better habits.

Wright

It's almost like saying, "Let's make all the mistakes in the laboratory before we put this thing in the air."

Covey

Right; and I also think what is necessary is a paradigm shift, which is analogous to having a correct map, say of a city or of a country. If people have an inaccurate paradigm of life, of other people, and of themselves it really doesn't make much difference what their behavior or habits or attitudes are. What they need is a correct paradigm—a correct map—that describes what's going on.

For instance, in the Middle Ages they used to heal people through bloodletting. It wasn't until Samuel Weiss and Pasteur and other empirical scientists discovered the germ theory that they realized for the first time they weren't dealing with the real issue. They realized why women preferred to use midwives who washed rather than doctors who didn't wash. They gradually got a new paradigm. Once you've got a new paradigm then your behavior and your attitude flow directly from it. If you have a bad paradigm or a bad map, let's say of a city, there's no way, no matter what your behavior or your habits or your attitudes are—how positive they are—you'll never be able to find the location you're looking for. This is why I believe that to change paradigms is far more fundamental than to work on attitude and behavior.

Wright

One of your seven habits of highly effective people is to "begin with the end in mind." If circumstances change and hardships or miscalculations occur, how does one view the end with clarity?

Covey

Many people think to begin with the end in mind means that you have some fixed definition of a goal that's accomplished and if changes come about you're not going to adapt to them. Instead, the "end in mind" you begin with is that you are going to create a flexible culture of high trust so that no matter what comes along you are going to do whatever it takes to accommodate that new change or that new reality and maintain a culture of high performance and high trust. You're talking more in terms of values and overall purposes that don't change, rather than specific strategies or programs that will have to change to accommodate the changing realities in the marketplace.

Wright

In this time of mistrust among people, corporations, and nations, for that matter, how do we create high levels of trust?

Covey

That's a great question and it's complicated because there are so many elements that go into the creating of a culture of trust. Obviously the most fundamental one is just to have trustworthy people. But that is not sufficient because what if the organization itself is misaligned?

For instance, what if you say you value cooperation but you really reward people for internal competition? Then you have a systemic or a structure problem that creates low trust inside the culture even though the people themselves are trustworthy. This is one of the insights of Edward Demming and the work he did. That's why he said that most problems are not personal—they're systemic. They're common caused. That's why you have to work on structure, systems, and processes to make sure that they institutionalize principle-centered values. Otherwise you could have good people with bad systems and you'll get bad results.

When it comes to developing interpersonal trust between people, it is made up of many, many elements such as taking the time to listen to other people, to understand them, and to see what is important to them. What we think is important to another may only be important to us, not to another. It takes empathy. You have to make and keep promises to them. You have to treat people with kindness and courtesy. You have to be completely honest and open. You have to live up to your commitments. You can't betray people behind their back. You can't badmouth them behind their back and sweet-talk them to their face. That will send out vibes of hypocrisy and it will be detected.

You have to learn to apologize when you make mistakes, to admit mistakes, and to also get feedback going in every direction as much as possible. It doesn't necessarily require formal forums—it requires trust between people who will be open with each other and give each other feedback.

Wright

My mother told me to do a lot of what you're saying now, but it seems that when I got in business I simply forgot.

Covey

Sometimes we forget, but sometimes culture doesn't nurture it. That's why I say unless you work with the institutionalizing—that means formalizing into structure, systems, and processing the values—you will not have a nurturing culture. You have to constantly work on that.

This is one of the big mistakes organizations make. They think trust is simply a function of being honest. That's only one small aspect. It's an important aspect, obviously, but there are so many other elements that go into the creation of a high-trust culture.

Wright

"Seek first to understand then to be understood" is another of your seven habits. Do you find that people try to communicate without really understanding what other people want?

Covey

Absolutely. The tendency is to project out of our own autobiography—our own life, our own value system—onto other people, thinking we know what they want. So we don't really listen to them. We pretend to listen, but we really don't listen from within their frame of reference. We listen from within our own frame of reference and we're really preparing our reply rather than seeking to understand. This is a very common thing. In fact, very few people have had any training in seriously listening. They're trained in how to read, write, and speak, but not to listen.

Reading, writing, speaking, and listening are the four modes of communication and they represent about two-thirds to three-fourths of our waking hours. About half of that time is spent listening, but it's the one skill people have not been trained in. People have had all this training in the other forms of communication. In a large audience of 1,000 people you wouldn't have more than twenty people who have had more than two weeks of training in listening. Listening is more than a skill or technique; you must listen within another's frame of reference. It takes tremendous courage to listen because you're at risk when you listen. You don't know what's going to happen; you're vulnerable.

Wright

Sales gurus always tell me that the number one skill in selling is listening.

Covey

Yes—listening from within the customer's frame of reference. That is so true. You can see that it takes some security to do that because you don't know what's going to happen.

Wright

With this book we're trying to encourage people to be better, to live better, and be more fulfilled by listening to the examples of our guest authors. Is there anything or anyone in your life that has made a difference for you and helped you to become a better person?

Covey

I think the most influential people in my life have been my parents. I think that what they modeled was not to make comparisons and harbor jealousy or to seek recognition. They were humble people.

I remember one time when my mother and I were going up in an elevator and the most prominent person in the state was also in the elevator. She knew him, but she spent her time talking to the elevator operator. I was just a little kid and I was so awed by the famous person. I said to her, "Why didn't you talk to the important person?" She said, "I was. I had never met him."

My parents were really humble, modest people who were focused on service and other people rather than on themselves. I think they were very inspiring models to me.

Wright

In almost every research paper I've ever read, those who write about people who have influenced their lives include three teachers in their top-five picks. My seventh-grade English teacher was the greatest teacher I ever had and she influenced me to no end.

Covey

Would it be correct to say that she saw in you probably some qualities of greatness you didn't even see in yourself?

Wright

Absolutely.

Covey

That's been my general experience—the key aspect of a mentor or a teacher is someone who sees in you potential that you don't even see in yourself. Those teachers/mentors treat you accordingly and eventually you come to see it in yourself. That's my definition of leadership or influence—communicating people's worth and potential so clearly that they are inspired to see it in themselves.

Wright

Most of my teachers treated me as a student, but she treated me with much more respect than that. As a matter of fact, she called me Mr. Wright, and I was in the seventh grade at the time. I'd never been addressed by anything but a nickname. I stood a little taller; she just made a tremendous difference.

Do you think there are other characteristics that mentors seem to have in common?

Covey

I think they are first of all good examples in their own personal lives. Their personal lives and their family lives are not all messed up—they come from a base of good character. They also are usually very confident and they take the time to do what your teacher did to you—to treat you with uncommon respect and courtesy.

They also, I think, explicitly teach principles rather than practices so that rules don't take the place of human judgment. You gradually come to have faith in your own judgment in making decisions because of the affirmation of such a mentor. Good mentors care about you—you can feel the sincerity of their caring. It's like the expression, "I don't care how much you know until I know how much you care."

Wright

Most people are fascinated with the new television shows about being a survivor. What has been the greatest comeback that you've made from adversity in your career or your life?

Covey

When I was in grade school I experienced a disease in my legs. It caused me to use crutches for a while. I tried to get off them fast and get back. The disease wasn't corrected yet so I went back on crutches for another year. The disease went to the other leg and I went on for another year. It essentially took me out of my favorite thing—athletics—and it took me more into being a student. So that was a life-defining experience, which at the time seemed very negative, but has proven to be the basis on which I've focused my life—being more of a learner.

Wright

Principle-centered learning is basically what you do that's different from anybody I've read or listened to.

Covey

The concept is embodied in the Far Eastern expression, "Give a man a fish, you feed him for the day; teach him how to fish, you feed him for a lifetime." When you teach principles that are universal and timeless, they don't belong to just any one person's religion or to a particular culture or geography. They seem to be timeless and universal like the ones we've been talking about here: trustworthiness, honesty, caring, service, growth, and development. These are universal principles. If you focus on these things, then little by little people become independent of you and then they start to believe in themselves and their own judgment becomes better. You don't need as many rules. You don't need as much bureaucracy and as many controls and you can empower people.

The problem in most business operations today—and not just business but non-business—is that they're using the industrial model in an information age. Arnold Toynbee, the great historian, said, "You can pretty well summarize all of history in four words: nothing fails like success." The industrial model was based on the asset of the machine. The information model is based on the asset of the person—the knowledge worker. It's an altogether different model. But the machine model was the main asset of the twentieth century. It enabled productivity to increase fifty times. The new asset is intellectual and social capital—the qualities of people and the quality of the relationship they have with each other. Like Toynbee said, "Nothing fails like success." The industrial model does not work in an information age. It requires a focus on the new wealth, not capital and material things.

A good illustration that demonstrates how much we were into the industrial model, and still are, is to notice where people are on the balance sheet. They're not found there. Machines are found there. Machines become investments. People are on the profit-and-loss statement and people are expenses. Think of that—if that isn't bloodletting.

Wright

It sure is.

When you consider the choices you've made down through the years, has faith played an important role in your life?

Covey

It has played an extremely important role. I believe deeply that we should put principles at the center of our lives, but I believe that God is the source of those principles. I did not invent them. I get credit sometimes for some of the Seven Habits material and some of the other things I've done, but it's really all based on principles that have been given by God to all of His children from the beginning of time. You'll find that you can teach these same principles from the sacred texts and the wisdom literature of almost any tradition. I think the ultimate source of that is God and that is one thing you can absolutely depend upon—"in God we trust."

Wright

If you could have a platform and tell our audience something you feel would help them or encourage them, what would you say?

Covey

I think I would say to put God at the center of your life and then prioritize your family. No one on their deathbed ever wished they had spent more time at the office.

Wright

That's right. We have come down to the end of our program and I know you're a busy person. I could talk with you all day, Dr. Covey.

Covey

It's good to talk with you as well and to be a part of this program. It looks like an excellent one that you've got going on here.

Wright

Thank you.

We have been talking today with Dr. Stephen R. Covey, cofounder and vice-chairman of Franklin Covey Company. He's also the author of The 7 Habits of Highly Effective People, which has been ranked as a number one bestseller by the New York Times, selling more than fourteen million copies in thirty-eight languages.

Dr. Covey, thank you so much for being with us today.

Covey

Thank you for the honor of participating.

ABOUT STEPHEN COVEY

Stephen R. Covey was recognized in 1996 as one of Time magazine's twenty-five most influential Americans and one of Sales and Marketing Management's top twenty-five power brokers. Dr. Covey is the author of several acclaimed books, including the international bestseller, The 7 Habits of Highly Effective People, named the number one Most Influential Business Book of the Twentieth Century, and other best sellers that include First Things First, Principle-Centered Leadership, (with sales exceeding one million) and The 7 Habits of Highly Effective Families.

Dr. Covey's newest book, The 8th Habit: From Effectiveness to Greatness, which was released in November 2004, rose to the top of several bestseller lists, including New York Times, Wall Street Journal, USA Today, Money, Business Week, Amazon.com, and Barnes & Noble.

Dr. Covey earned his undergraduate degree from the University of Utah, his MBA from Harvard, and completed his doctorate at Brigham Young University. While at Brigham Young University, he served as assistant to the President and was also a professor of Business Management and Organizational Behavior. He received the National Fatherhood Award in 2003, which, as the father of nine and grandfather of forty-four, he says is the most meaningful award he has ever received.

Dr. Covey currently serves on the board of directors for the Points of Light Foundation. Based in Washington, D.C., the Foundation, through its partnership with the Volunteer Center National Network, engages and mobilizes millions of volunteers from all walks of life—businesses, nonprofits, faith-based organizations, low-income communities, families, youth, and older adults—to help solve serious social problems in thousands of communities.

To Contact Dr. Stephen R. Covey...
Visit www.stephencovey.com.

ROADMAP to SUCCESS 3

An interview with ...

RICK WNUK

David Wright (Wright)

Today we're talking with Rick Wnuk. Rick is a corporate speaker and sales consultant who speaks on the topic of "Be REAL Selling: Connecting Your Way to Success." It's his belief that once we're real with ourselves we can effortlessly "Be Real" with others, enabling us to naturally connect. As a result, we differentiate ourselves, establish genuine relationships, and achieve success.

Rick has developed results-oriented behaviors that teach us to "Be Real" with others and ourselves that can be immediately applied to provide breakthrough results. He uses the word "REAL" as an acronym to introduce key principles that guide internal and external selling behaviors. He speaks passionately on the topic, as Being Real enabled him to achieve his success both professionally and personally.

He has more than twenty years of sales experience with a background in sales, consulting, and years of experience mentoring and coaching sales personnel to success. In addition to his speaking engagements, his consulting firm works with organizations to accelerate and optimize sales performance.

Rick, welcome to *Roadmap to Success*.

As a speaker and sales consultant, you collaborate with a wide spectrum of executives, organizations, and industries. What impact has technology had on evolving the role of the sales professional?

Wnuk

Today's business landscape is constantly changing, as advances in technology move at warp speed and so much knowledge is at our fingertips. As a result, the role of the sales professional has evolved from that of a consultant, offering information and solutions, to today's role—more of a strategic advisor. As this model continues to evolve, the primary point of differentiation is the sales professional and his or her ability to establish genuine relationships. Having this ability is essential as relationships drive business!

Wright

If the sales professional is the primary point of differentiation, how can we establish genuine relationships that differentiate us from all of the others?

Wnuk

Simply put, the answer is to "Be Real"! Sales is now about more than positive thinking, competitive strategies, value add, and value propositions—it's about making *real* connections. The majority of salespeople have the *desire and skills* to connect. However, the problem is not lack of desire; it's the application of the skills. This is not something that is taught in school. It's not a common topic for training and development. The bottom line is that we simply lack a road map to guide us toward establishing genuine relationships that will help us to differentiate ourselves.

Wright

You mention the importance of making real connections. How do you define connections and how often do we make them?

Wnuk

Consider research from the University of Alabama that indicates we spend approximately one third of our waking hours connecting with others. This means that on a daily basis we spend five to seven waking hours engaged with others. Connections may be a brief conversation or a relationship that spans years. It may be a short conversation with a stranger where you connect on a topic, perspective, thought, or even a visual connection such as a smile. Connecting may occur with a new client who shares similar values, strategies, and business principles.

The question is not how often you connect, however; it's how real you are with yourself and others when connecting. Similar to defining success, connecting is defined by the individual. You define it; you own it! For me, connecting occurs when my intentions are unconditional and pure, where I am not acting a role or persona—where I am my authentic self. This is what I refer to as *"Being Real!"*

For others, it may be similar to when two magnets are drawn together—when you're completely at ease with what's around you, when you lose track of time because you're excited about where a conversation may go, when you're in the moment, giving complete attention to your thoughts, or when you're in a conversation sharing different perspectives and you're completely open to other points of view, even if you don't agree with them.

Wright

You mention that we need to *"be real."* Aren't people always *real?*

Wnuk

Many of us believe we are *real.* However, the truth is that it's common for people to create personas that we act out personally, socially, and professionally. For example, if we want to protect ourselves, perhaps we assume a role where we don't communicate our feelings. If we have a fear of failing, we may assume a "can't do" persona, where we communicate all the reasons why a positive outcome is not likely. We adopt these personas, which are often built on misguided belief systems, to mask our genuine selves, hide our fears, and protect our feelings. They are simply an act—manipulating our belief system, snuffing out our genuine selves, and inhibiting our ability to connect.

I'm familiar with personas, as at one time I had several. They protected me from my fear of failure. Many of us adopt personas that conceal our fears, impeding our ability to genuinely connect and differentiate ourselves.

Being a speaker and sales consultant, I'm afforded the opportunity to work and collaborate with many business and sales professionals, many of whom create personas that are based on their achievements where success is simply measured by the outcome. Unfortunately, this focus blinds them to many opportunities to genuinely connect. Combine this belief with consistently focusing on what we didn't do well versus congratulating ourselves on moving forward, and the result is a belief system where there is no peace and no acknowledgement of success.

The outcome of such a belief system are acts and personas that are so complex they lead us further and further away from our authentic self, further from our ability to connect, further from our ability to differentiate ourselves, and further from our success. The analogy I use is that of a hummingbird and an eagle. Those who are not being *real* move their wings like a hummingbird trying to achieve success. Those who follow my Be REAL Road Map fly not like a hummingbird, but like an eagle—simply gliding along with power, enjoying the journey, at peace with their decisions.

Wright

What is your "Be REAL Road Map"?

Wnuk

There are many roads to success—it's our choice to maximize each road we take. It's unfortunate that many of us don't see the many roads. We selectively and many times subconsciously shield ourselves from opportunities, experiences, and connections that naturally present themselves. Perhaps we shield ourselves because of our fears, a subconscious desire to stay in our comfort zone, or simply to feel safe. What we often don't realize is that to achieve our desired success, we must embrace the journey and expand our comfort zone. The Be REAL Road Map is a guide to be used as you travel the many roads that may lead to your success. The guide is based on both my personal experiences as well as collaborations with business leaders, clients, sales professionals, and development experts.

The Road Map doesn't start at Go or the Starting Line. It all starts internally! You are at the center of your beliefs, actions, and relationships. The first step of the Road Map guides you through Being REAL internally. Once we're real with ourselves, we can seamlessly and genuinely connect with others. This is sustainable—acting through personas is not!

Wright

What are the key principles of your Be REAL Road Map that guide us internally?

Wnuk

Using the word REAL as an acronym, the following are the key principles:

Release the Outcome
Emotions: Recognize and Communicate
Accountability
Likeable

Release the Outcome

To genuinely connect, we must first realize that the end result does not define who we are: it's the journey that we need to maximize. This is difficult for many sales professionals because we tend to focus on the black and white of reaching the goal or not. The reality is that *what we learn on our journey* defines who we are, not the outcome. Many of the decisions we face on our journey are daunting. However, we become the person we are meant to be as we elevate our ability to trust ourselves and build on that trust to accumulate knowledge, skills, courage, wisdom, and the perseverance to move forward. As a result, we commit ourselves to expanding our comfort zone.

To put this principle into context of sales, let's use the example of a sales professional for whom a common goal is to prospect for new business. It's safe to say that the majority of sales professionals prefer not to cold-call to find this new business. However, at times, cold calling is necessary. This is the decision the sales professional may have to make, the path he or she commits to take.

Regardless of the path, you should embrace the principle that there are always opportunities to Be REAL in any situation, even one we do not want to be in. In this prospecting scenario, Releasing the Outcome translates to understanding that a "no" is an opportunity for professional growth. The sales professional can learn to trust that if the cold-call is rejected, the prospect is rejecting the service or product, not the sales professional. He or she can embrace the fact that although the desired outcome may not be achieved, there is value in the journey. In this scenario, the value may be an improved "pitch," another business model to engage prospects, refined positioning statements, awareness of a new best practice, courage, visibility to trends, or something else. The point is, we can't control the thoughts and feelings of another. What we can control is our ability to value the journey and value our thoughts, feelings, and beliefs!

I have firsthand knowledge that you don't gain this trust by simply achieving an end result—it's gained from the journey. It's gained from learning from the failures, from the wisdom you gain from connecting with others, and it's gained by connecting with your genuine self. Releasing the outcome means you embrace the principle that the value is in the journey, not the end result.

Similar to the cold-calling example, many of us have flawed perceptions that results are an indication of success—results define who we are—but this is not the case.

I'll reference a recent client engagement to further illustrate this point. Lee and Joe are sales representatives for a large software firm calling on the financial services industry. Each of them have an annual revenue goal of $5 million. Joe is in a proven territory. He simply maintains existing customers and has little desire to step out of his comfort zone to expand his skills. At year's end, he has achieved his $5 million revenue goal. At the end of the period, he's the same person with the same skills, experiences, and perceptions as at the beginning of the year.

On the other hand, Lee is in a new territory, one that the company never penetrated. Lee designs and executes a new business model, one that is projected to generate five times more revenue on an annual basis than the company's traditional model. Due to the structure of the financial model, he falls short of his annual revenue goal. However, along the way, he maximized the journey—he embraced challanges to refine the model, he stepped out of his comfort zone, he gained valuable skills along the way, and he trusted himself. As a result, he elevated his game and will leverage the experience to achieve greater success in the future. The question becomes, which one truly succeeded in his pursuit of success?

To Release the Outcome, we need to frequently ask ourselves: am I doing the best I can, am I pushing myself, am I expanding my comfort zone, am I aware of the opportunities that are presenting themselves?

Step out of the box! Let's not stay in the box of self-limiting thinking and behaviors. Let's commit ourselves to releasing the outcome and to enjoy the journey as we take it.

Emotions: Recognize and Communicate

At the cost of many genuine relationships, many of us (and I was one of them) don't realize the significant value in recognizing and communicating emotions. We were never taught how to recognize and express emotions. As a matter of fact, many of us are taught to suppress our emotions! We are told to be strong and stoic, to never show signs of weakness. I believe the opposite: that strong people have the awareness to recognize and communicate their emotions. It's the unfortunate person who doesn't have such awareness. As a result, many miss the opportunity to establish and truly feel genuine connections.

If we can't connect with ourselves on an emotional level, how can we expect others to connect with us? Many times we simply don't have the awareness or the emotional vocabulary to recognize and communicate our emotions. To Be Real, we need to have the capacity to recognize our own feelings and those of others. Increasing and improving our capacity in this area is similar to learning or refining a new language. We can build a vocabulary of emotions, enabling us to easily recognize and communicate feelings. To expand our emotional vocabulary, we can create a list of emotions and express them on a daily basis. Every morning, ask yourself how you feel. Answer with an emotion. Ask yourself if you want to change it. If you do, ask how you can change it—it's your feeling—you own it and you can decide what to do with it.

Does this sound basic and sophomoric? If it does, it probably means your emotional vocabulary needs to be expanded. As a result of that expansion, I'm confident that you'll learn to use your vocabulary to establish many genuine connections.

A great situation in which to apply your new language is the morning greeting, where we typically exchange the "hello." How genuine is this typical exchange:

"How are you this morning"?

"Great! And you?"

"Great! Have a good day."

Such conversations are not only transactional, they are of no value—of little connection. Having the awareness and vocabulary enables us to open up and understand that's it okay to be vulnerable. The next morning greeting, tell the person how you are feeling. For example, if you are very excited because you have a keynote to deliver or that you are happy because you met with a satisfied client – tell them! Expressing ourselves with words such as excited, eager, disappointed—with emotions—are connection points!

Many times in sales we feel trapped in situations, relationhips and conversations. Rather than being trapped in or losing control of the situation, one should strive to have self-awareness. Self-awareness is the first step toward identifying and changing our behaviors. Similar to Being Real, there are two lenses with which to view self-awareness: internal and external.

Internally, the awareness enables us to understand ourselves and use it to monitor our behavior. For example, individuals who have emotional awareness recognize the events and interactions that trigger certain emotions. In a sales environment, it may be one of rejection or blind optimism. As a result, they can proactively identify, process, and communicate their feelings and propose recommendations to move a sales opportunity or conversation forward.

The external element is the ability to recognize opportunities to express empathy. Empathy means having the awareness and understanding of the feelings of another, and possessing empathy enables us to recognize the perspectives of others. Recognizing the feelings of others and communicating on an emotional level provides the opportunity to genuinely connect. In a selling environment, realize that 98 percent of us buy products or services emotionally and justify the decision logically. Therefore sales professionals need to connect to the emotional reasons buyers are interested in their product or service. Furthermore, they have to establish a genuine connection because once buyers make an investment, they stop responding emotionally and focus on the fundamental and rational business reasons why an investment was made.

As you follow the Be REAL Road Map, connect with others by learning the language, paying attention to how you and others are feeling in any moment, and exercising the ability to "read" and interpret the feeling.

Accountability

To Be REAL, we need to be accountable—to ourselves and to others. This accountability is based on our ability to move forward to our success and with our connections. To reinforce our commitments, a road map guides us as we move forward and redirects us when we get off track. If we truly desire to elevate ourselves to another level, we need to have a compass that leads us to our desired result. In support of your commitment, visualize being accountable to a process, visualize doing the hard work, embrace the hard work, and enjoy the journey! Feel success, act out your success, and visualize the process that you took to get there.

For many of us, identifying the goal is the easy part. Defining the path and holding ourselves accountable is the difficult part. To embrace accountability, regularly ask yourself if you have taken a step forward to achieve your definition of success. If so, congratulate yourself for taking the step—even if it's the smallest of steps. If not, ask yourself what step you can take today or tomorrow that will enable you to move forward.

If you find that you are not holding yourself accountable, ask yourself how important the goal is. Perhaps the goal is not important to the genuine you but is one that aligns to a persona. Furthermore, ask yourself if and how you are nurturing your relationhips? Performing these self-checks will enable you to move toward a success that is better aligned to the authentic you.

Likeable

Bottom line, before someone is going to connect with you, you have to like yourself. Think for a moment: on a daily basis, who do you have the most conversations with? Is it your partner, your children, your parents, or your colleagues?

You may be surprised to learn that it's yourself! Research indicates that we have thousands of conversations per day with ourselves. The question becomes: what are we saying? Is it negative self-talk where we are beating ourselves up? Are we beating ourselves up because we allowed ourselves to reach out of our comfort zone and believe we failed, that we didn't achieve our professional goal, that we made a fool of ourselves, that we communicated our feelings and got hurt, that others may now perceive us as weak? The list goes on and on. The fact is we control our beliefs, we control our thoughts, we control ourselves, and we choose to like ourselves.

To put this into context, have you ever talked to a child or a colleague and you were yelling at the top of your voice? Were your words like daggers repeatedly plunging into the other person's body? Were you telling the person things like how stupid his or her actions were and that only a complete idiot would do that? Would you do this? Of course not!

The reality is that many of us talk to ourselves like this on a daily basis! To what end? What does it do? What lesson does it teach? It simply confines us to our comfort zone—our box.

The takeaway from this message is to realize that we are all human. Yes, we make mistakes, but we have the opportunity to experience them and to learn from them. Going forward, we need to stretch ourselves, expand our comfort zone, and congratulate ourselves when we take a step forward, regardless of whether it was a positive or negative experience. The fact remains that if we're not failing, we're not stretching ourselves—we're not moving forward toward our success. Remember that progress is accelerated more from a negative experience than a positive one. Again, we are not robots—we are imperfect humans, so encourage yourself, congratulate yourself, and like yourself.

Wright

What are the principles to the Be REAL Road Map that guide us externally?

Wnuk

At one time, it was my belief that we could act out several personas dependant on the situation and still establish genuine relationships. However, what I discovered is that although one can be very successful in certain situations many of the relationships developed are superficial as personas can mask their genuine self. We have to embrace and understand that we are at the core of all of our connections—we are at the core regardless if we are connecting on a social, professional, or casual platform. The point is that we first have to be Real with ourselves, which will enable us to be Real with others to genuinely connect. With the principles of Being REAL acting as the foundation, the following are the key principles to Be REAL with others:

Relevant
Engaging
Attitude
Linked In

Relevant

How many times have you been in a conversation where you are focused on topic A and the other person is focused on topic Z? Is there a connection? Is there a value exchange? To effectively connect, we must be relevant.

To illustrate the point, I'll share a story with you of a small child who was raising funds for charity during the holidays. He practiced his introduction and his pitch, and he was prepared and confident. His plan was to go neighborhood to neighborhood selling Christmas cards. He outlined his approach, deciding on the neighborhoods that he was going to visit—one for each day.

The first two days went great. Unfortunately, he struggled for the next two days and couldn't understand the reason for the change.

That evening, he sat down with his parents to review the first four days. He wanted to understand why the first two days were great and the next two didn't work out as well. He was committed to maximizing the journey. When discussing his charity work, his parents first congratulated him on his effort. Then they asked which neighborhoods he had visited. As he was answering the question, the realization hit him. He wasn't relevant! The first two neighborhoods he went to were primarily Catholic, whereas the second two were primarily Jewish. The principle behind this story is that in order to connect, we have to be relevant.

I believe in many of the principles developed by Everett Rogers specific to the stages of adoption. I use several of these stages to illustrate and act as a guide to being relevant. Use them as a guide as you introduce a best practice or business strategy, an idea, solution, feeling, or thought. They are:

- Awareness—At this stage, the individual is exposed to an idea, innovation, or thought.
- Understanding—At this stage, the individual becomes interested in the idea and seeks additional information.
- Acceptance—At this stage, the individual mentally applies it to his or her present and anticipated future situation.
- Commitment—At this final stage, the individual decides to continue the full use of the idea, thought, or innovation.

The key point is to first seek to understand where your audience may be on the topic and align your connection to where they are. Aligning with your audience will ensure that you're relevant, thus enabling you to connect.

You also need to ensure that you have relevant knowledge. In other words, do you have the knowledge to be relevant and of value to your audience? As we continue to pursue success, we should all ask ourselves each day what steps we are taking to increase our knowledge.

Additionally, being knowledgeable supports our effort to be Engaging.

Engaging

Connecting with others first requires that we're open to a conversation. Being open for a conversation means we are approachable, and being approachable can come from a simple smile or displaying positive body language. A perfect illustration of this is what happens when we step into an elevator. Typically, everyone stares straight ahead looking at the numbers as though something is going to change. Next time, look around and ask yourself how approachable you are. How approachable are others? What body language are people displaying? What about their facial features? Our usual elevator behavior is a perfect example of how *not* to be approachable.

Once engaged, we need to be open and have the awareness that all real connections are of interest. This awareness enables us to transform transactional conversations to transformational conversations. In many conversations, we know exactly what we want to say and how we'll say it. We know precisely where we are leading the conversations and why—it's like an actor reading a script. Unfortunately, when a transactional conversation is over, we merely read the script. We're the same person we were at the beginning of the conversation. The conversations are referred to as "transactional" because they're simply an exchange. I refer to them as a missed opportunity—a missed opportunity to Be REAL—to connect and to enjoy the journey.

As we become Real, we'll have the skills to transform transactional conversations to transformational conversations. They can be a marked change, expansion, or reinforcement of our beliefs, knowledge, and behaviors. These are the genuine connections where we don't know what the outcome will be, what solutions we'll find, what experiences or perspectives will be shared, what problems we'll be addressing, or even who we'll be or how the conversation may impact us in the future. The point is to maximize every opportunity to genuinely connect with others, regardless if it's the CEO of your best client or the person standing on line in front of you. You'll not only transform your conversations but you'll also transform yourself.

As a sales professional, strive to be engaging by being motivated by the value your client will receive from your offering rather than the "reward" you'll receive from selling it.

Attitude

Achieving and maintaining a positive attitude is key. What I know through experience is that negative people are a mental and physical drain. Stay away from the negative blender and connect with people who have a positive attitude. It's contagious—and it's great to catch it. Positive people see opportunities, and other people want to be around them and want to connect with them. Positive people want to grow and step out of their comfort zones—they would rather try and fail than not try at all. With a positive attitude, I know that I am achieving my success, and I know that you can also truly achieve your success.

An analogy that I use to reinforce a positive attitude is the mood ring from the 1970s. The concept of the mood ring is that the ring changes color in response to the attitude or emotional state of the wearer. The lighter the color the more positive he or she is, whereas the darker the color, the more negative the person is.

When in a conversation, visualize the mood ring. Ask yourself what your color is—is it light or dark? What is causing you to feel this way? Map back to your emotions. Furthermore, ask yourself what is the color of the ring of the person with whom you are connecting? Keying in to this awareness will enable you to establish genuine connections. Stay positive and trust yourself because your attitude is contagious to others and to yourself.

Linked In

The primary principle behind being linked in within multiple networks is based on the opportunity to connect in the areas of knowledge, perspectives, individuals, dreams, and emotions. This principle is supported by the work of Mark Granovetter, an American sociologist in the area of "the strength of weak ties." His research stated that to find new information or insights, we have to look beyond our "clique." The premise is to seek out new insights and ideas because one will not gain them from a static comfort zone. As you connect outside of your clique, share ideas and best practices because you will naturally be linked in.

To expand our networks, we should take the fundamental approach of not expecting anything in return! Expand your network by exchanging ideas, by introducing people who may have similar interests or who may benefit from knowing one another. Do it because you genuinely have an interest in helping others—ask for nothing in return. Think of a boomerang—the majority of the time it comes back around. And if it doesn't, embrace the fact that it was pretty cool to throw it.

Wright

How does one define success?

Wnuk

Our success is uniquely defined by each one of us. There is not a standard definition because each of us is unique in our thoughts, dreams, and skills.

The Be REAL Road Map is a guide—a guide that will help lead us to our unique success. Success is defined by each one of us in our own unique way. My definition of success is different from yours. My success is simply having the ability to make decisions without fear and without being paralyzed by the potential of negative outcomes. This enables me to pursue my dreams and my passion and to genuinely connect. In other words, I fly like the eagle as I enjoy my journey!

You own your success. You own your journey. You own your connections. You now own the Road Map that will enable you to connect for success. Regardless of your definition of success, enjoy the journey because tomorrow is simply a gift—not a given.

Wright

What proactive behaviors can one take to Be REAL?

Wnuk

One of many gifts that we all have is that we have the opportunity to choose if and how we connect with ourselves and others. The question becomes, whichever path you decide to take, ask yourself on a daily basis "Are you Being REAL?"

To help answer this question, the Be REAL Assessment aids in creating such awareness:

Be REAL Selling Assessment

1. Are you motivated more by:
    a. the "reward" you will receive or
    b. the value that you deliver?
2. At a networking function do you:
    a. make a referral expecting something in return or
    b. make a referral with the belief it will help someone?
3. What defines you:
    a. your achievements or
    b. your beliefs and actions?

4. Do you mentally track what a person may owe you?
    a. yes
    b. no
5. Do you typically drive the conversation toward your desired outcome?
    a. yes
    b. no
6. In a casual conversation, do you let the conversation:
    a. direct it to your desired outcome or
    b. let it naturally flow?
7. Is it a failure if you didn't achieve your desired outcome, but you gained invaluable knowledge during the pursuit?
    a. yes
    b. no
8. Do you believe:
    a. you are not "referral worthy" or
    b. that you are "referral worthy"?
9. Throughout the day, do you typically exhibit
    a. negative body language or
    b. positive body language?
10. In a business situation do you:
    a. rarely express yourself to ensure your needs are met or
    b. almost always express yourself to ensure your needs are met?
11. How often do you push your comfort zone?
    a. rarely
    b. often
12. When rejected do you:
    a. withdraw into your comfort zone or
    b. embrace and learn from the experience?
13. What's your belief:
    a. I have to do it or
    b. I have the opportunity to do it?
14. What best describes your perspective:
    a. results before relationships or
    b. relationships before results?
15. Is it your belief that:
    a. you should connect with others before you connect with yourself or
    b. you should connect with yourself before you connect with others?
16. Are your actions and behaviors driven by:
    a. what you think is right or

b.   what you believe is right?
17. In a conversation, are you thinking of:
    a.   what you are going to say next or
    b.   are you in the moment truly listening?
18. In specific situations, do you act out personas that guide your behaviors?
    a.   yes
    b.   no
19. Typically, do you focus on:
    a.   the things you didn't do well or
    b.   do you congratulate yourself on moving forward?
20. Do you work through self-limiting thinking and behaviors?
    a.   no
    b.   yes
21. Do you realize the value in recognizing and communicating emotions?
    a.   no
    b.   yes
22. Do you have the awareness to "read" and interpret the feelings and perspective of others?
    a.   no
    b.   yes
23. When you're not holding yourself accountable to a goal, do you ask how important it is?
    a.   no
    b.   yes
24. Do you have to like yourself before someone else is going to like you?
    a.   no
    b.   yes
25. Do you first seek to understand where your audience is on a topic prior to talking about it?
    a.   no
    b.   yes
26. Do you prefer a transactional conversation that is simply an exchange of information or a transformational conversation where you don't know what the outcome will be or even how the conversation may impact you in the future?
    a.   transactional
    b.   transformational
27. Envision wearing a mood ring that changes color in response to your attitude. Typically, what is your daily color?
    a.   Lighter because this indicates a positive can do attitude or

   b.   darker because this indicates a negative I can't attitude.
28. Are your actions driven by
   a.   your desired outcome or
   b.   by a genuine interest in helping others?
29. Tomorrow is simply a gift—not a given.
   a.   disagree
   b.   agree
30. Do you believe your behaviors, actions, and beliefs are Real?
   a.   no
   b.   yes

Guide

- More than twenty-three "b" responses: You are well on your way to being Real. Continue to embrace the journey.

- Seventeen to twenty-three "b" responses: The foundation is in place. Embrace the message that a journey begins with the first step.

- Less than seventeen "b" responses: Focus on connecting and trusting yourself.

ABOUT RICK WNUK

In today's competitive selling environment, the sales professional is the primary differentiator. Sales professionals must embrace the principles of connecting with themselves and others to stand apart.

Rick Wnuk is a corporate speaker and sales consultant who speaks on the topic of "Be REAL Selling: Connecting Your Way to Success." It's his belief that once we're *REAL* with ourselves we can effortlessly *Be REAL* with others enabling us to naturally connect. As a result, we achieve balance, differentiate ourselves, and establish genuine relationships.

Rick has developed the specific methodology and results-oriented behaviors to *Be REAL* with ourselves and others that can be immediately applied to provide breakthrough results. He speaks passionately on the topic because *Being REAL* enabled him to achieve success both professionally and personally.

In addition to his speaking and coaching engagements, his consulting firm works with organizations to accelerate and optimize sales performance. He is also a frequent contributor on sales-related topics to *Selling Power* magazine, EyesOnSales, WebEx Communications and the American Management Association.

He has more than twenty years of sales experience with a background in consulting and years of experience mentoring and coaching sales personnel to success.

Rick Wnuk
Be REAL Selling
919.412.8922
rick@berealselling.com
www.berealselling.com

ROADMAP to SUCCESS 4

An interview with ...

ED ABEL

David Wright (Wright)

Today, we're talking with Ed Abel. He is an iPEC-Certified Business Coach who turned a $5,000 loan into a 36 million dollar business. He is the creator and founder of Abel Business Institute, which offers successful, proven business strategies and much needed support to entrepreneurs, *Skillpreneurs*®, and business proprietors, as well as existing larger company executives who want to take their business to a higher level. Ed is a trusted advisor and confidant to business owners who are serious about tackling both typical and complex business issues, and who welcome honest assessments and feedback about their business processes and the decisions they make. He is also the director of the business division at iPEC-Coaching School.

In addition to mentoring and educating other coaches, he created a ready-to-use package of tried-and-true business processes so other coaches can use the program to build their own client base and grow their businesses.

Ed created and leads what he calls "MBA Groups." The MBA stands for "Mastermind Business Alliance." MBA groups help business owners achieve success. However, what separates an MBA group from a standard business meeting is the environment Ed provides to his MBA group members. The environment of an MBA group meeting is one where camaraderie exists, information flows, knowledge is shared, purpose is achieved, and everyone leaves the meeting feeling more enlightened, committed, confident, and less alone than when they entered. Based on his experience as a successful business owner, Ed created a series of seminar and training programs to help coaches, consultants, entrepreneurs, professionals, and business owners alike. He also talks to organizations and associations, sharing his insider wisdom about the ups and downs of owning your own business.

Ed, welcome to *Roadmap for Success.*

Ed Abel (Abel)

Thank you.

Wright

As an IV nurse, you borrowed $5,000 to turn an idea into a 36 million dollar business that employed 585 people. What is the most important lesson you learned about starting and growing your own business?

Abel

Well, most people who start their own businesses think they are entrepreneurs. They usually have the passion and drive that are characteristic of an entrepreneur, but it takes more than passion and drive to be an entrepreneur. If you've never built a business, you lack the necessary skills to sustain and grow it; I learned that lesson while building my own business. After years of trial, error, and missteps, when I look back, it was clear that when I launched my business I was really a *Skillpreneur*® not an entrepreneur.

Wright

So, please tell our readers, what is a *Skillpreneur?*

Abel

A *Skillpreneur* is a technical expert in a specific art, skill, trade, or technique. *Skillpreneurs* have a talent or a trained skill, and through training and experience they've developed their skill so they can in fact become experts in their field or industry. But because they have little or no experience building a business; they are really *Skillpreneurs,* they aren't prepared to be business owners yet.

Take an accountant or a hairdresser: they could be top in their fields, but what do they know about launching and building a business? So these *Skillpreneurs* go off on their own and start a business because they believe they can do it better than the company for which they work. That's how most "Skillpreneurs" start out. They have an "I'm going to go into business because I can do it better" attitude. Unfortunately, they learn that what they really know is how to work *in* their business, not *on* their business.

I was a great IV nurse, but I knew nothing about hiring, training, financing, billing, inventory control, payroll, quality assurance, sales, marketing, or management. I had the "I'm going to go into business because I can do it better" attitude. I had no idea what being "in business" really entailed.

Wright

You're saying that one needs more than a skill or a set of skills to start and grow a successful business. What do entrepreneurs bring to the table that *Skillpreneurs* do not?

Abel

Entrepreneurs bring more than a skill or experience in a particular field to their business. First, they bring a vision. They have the vision of their product and/or service, and they understand the market it will serve. In addition:

- They have a mission statement that reflects their purpose, their image, and the social responsibility for their business.
- They have goals. They see where they want to take the business in one year, three years, and five years down the road—and are willing to change direction.
- They are leaders. They actually understand that they're going to lead their business, not have the business lead them. Business owners who are stuck in the day-to-day tasks of running their business are not leading; they are simply trying to survive.

So *Skillpreneurs* bring a skill and not much else to the table. *Skillpreneurs* are their business. They follow their business, while trained business owners and entrepreneurs lead their business.

Wright

So what advice do you have for *Skillpreneurs* who want to start their own business?

Abel

Assuming that *Skillpreneurs* have the idea and the passion for the business, they need to look at the big picture. Besides business decisions, they need to look at their stage in life. Before moving forward, they need to consider the following:

- Are they single or married?
- Do they have children?
- What will they do for income until the business really starts making money?
- How much will it cost to start the business?
- How will the work get done?
- Who will do the work?

There are many things to consider. The bottom line is they will need lots of support. Support is the key; you can't build or grow a successful business by yourself.

Wright

With so many things to consider, what is the first step business proprietors need to take along the road to success?

Abel

They need an idea and a plan—a business plan. That's really where it starts. Once you have the idea, you then need the plan. What happens with a lot of budding business owners is that they get a million dollar idea and they run with it. Their enthusiasm drives them until they run into the first problem, which could be a simple problem or a major roadblock, but they're stuck and they don't know where to turn.

Now, if they have a business plan, they have a road map to guide them. It doesn't mean they won't have problems or challenges, but with a plan in place, they have direction. They might have to change direction, but they won't get lost. A business plan is a detailed record of your intentions for your business. If it's not written, you're flying by the seat of your pants. It's only a matter of time before you risk falling apart and losing your business.

Wright

As you grew from *Skillpreneur* to a business leader, what action propelled you forward more than anything else?

Abel

Establishing goals and creating an action plan were my two key ingredients that drove my success. My business started as a dream. What makes the dream come true is turning it into a goal. A goal is a dream with a deadline. Business owners need to think about:

- Short-term goals,
- Mid-term goals,
- Long-term goals,
- What the big picture looks like,
- Where you want to be in five years, in ten years, etc.

Goals need to be specific. You develop a master plan based on the goals, then you develop your mile-markers or your midterm goals so you can measure your progress along the way. Now that I coach business owners, I can say with confidence that when business owners who lack a plan and goals get stuck, they don't know what to do. As a result, they never achieve their primary goal of running a successful business. They never achieve their dream.

Wright

Ed, can you share with the readers what you have found to be essential elements for business success?

Abel

I sure can, I have ten, and I call them the

10 Commandments for Business Success

1. Thou shall work on thy business, not in thy business. This determines whether you are an entrepreneur or a *Skillpreneur*. If you're an entrepreneur, you're leading your business, but if you're a *Skillpreneur*, you need to find someone who will help you lead your business—or you will get stuck.

2. Thou shall act, not react. Leaders act, *Skillpreneurs* react. This leads to: do you manage your day or does your day manage you? This is about effective time management. Put simply: are you getting done what needs to get done or does the day dictate what you do?

3. Thou shall duplicate thyself. At least double your productivity by creating a powerful support team. As I said earlier, you can't do this alone. Nobody builds a business alone. One of the keys to success for growth and development is to have a support team that works with you and helps you create your vision.

4. Thou shall ask thy clients to work for thee. This is one of my favorites because when your clients brag about you, they become your best marketing tool. You want your clients to be raving fans. I often ask entrepreneurs and small business owners: how many of your clients will paint their face and stand out in your colors in twenty-degree weather and brag about your team?

5. Thou shall hire money. Like an employee, make your money work for you. Most people have no idea how to make money work for them. They don't know how to manage it. They don't know how to read a cash flow statement. They really don't understand the value of the money and how to make it work for them.

6. Thou shall understand, know, and master the six Ps:
    1. Passion. If you're coming into business and you don't have passion, you're not going to survive.
    2. Patience. You have to be patient because the process takes time.
    3. Persistence. Since you never know how close to the finish line you really are, you need to be persistent.

4. Positive attitude. Starting and growing a business is full of challenges. A positive attitude goes a long way.

5. Planning. Plan a strategic way to leverage how to use time, money, energy, and other resources to minimize effort and maximize results.

6. Practice. Yes, practice. By practice I mean learning, learning, and more learning about each and every step of your business development.

7. Thou shall not manage, because managing is controlling. What you want to do is lead; leading is empowering.

8. Thou shall never deliver what thou hast promised. You must deliver more than you promise! Every one of your clients should walk away thinking that each one has taken away more than was expected. When you give more than expected, you create value, and your business will grow and thrive.

9. Thou shall continue to take care of thy most important asset—thyself. The key to success is investing most of your time in you. Make sure you take care of yourself—make sure that you eat, rest, exercise, and take stock of what you are doing on a daily basis so that you can do a better job of managing. Continue training programs, coaching and educating yourself.

10. Walk the talk. Make sure that you do what you say you're going to do. If you don't, you'll be history.

Wright

Those are great. As a business coach and entrepreneur, what other success secrets can you share with *Skillpreneurs* or anyone who wants to be a successful business owner?

Abel

Business owners who are successful know how to delegate. They know they can go only so far on their own. In fact, entrepreneurs look forward to the day when they can hire employees or independent consultants so they can focus on growing their business.

Successful business leaders also recognize the value in hiring those who possess the skills they themselves lack. *Skillpreneurs*, on the other hand, typically believe that by hiring a staff or working with independent contractors, they are giving up control of their business. But by refusing to recognize they need help, the only thing *Skillpreneurs* give up is the ability to grow their business.

Another principle successful business owners understand is the value of creating systems. In fact, the Internet, software programs, and the ability to automate just about every aspect of the business are some of the greatest gifts to entrepreneurs. Leaders teach their people to create systems because they know it's crazy to do the same thing over and over again. Because *Skillpreneurs* are caught up in the day-to-day tasks of running their business, they go crazy trying to keep up with the tasks that can be systemized. We created a unique day and time management system to solve this problem: The Daily Do-It Dashboard."

Wright

So in your work with business owners, what do you see as one of the biggest roadblocks to success?

Abel

The number one killer for most business owners is poor time management. Time is our most precious resource in personal and business pursuits. Once you use it, it's gone—whether you used it wisely or fritted it away. This is especially true when people don't set priorities and they lack organization. As a result, they procrastinate and do nothing. To have a successful business, the absolute number one key to making the most of your time is to be organized and focused. When you do that, you're on your road to success.

Wright

Earlier you said support is vital to business success. Would you expand on that by telling our readers the type of support that fosters and encourages success?

Abel

The number one thing I find most business owners struggle with is thinking that they should do it all on their own. They think they should have all the answers. But when you look at a business, there are multiple areas that call for expertise, and you can't be an expert in everything.

For instance, if you never did bookkeeping, why spend time learning QuickBooks? Instead, delegate by hiring an independent bookkeeper or accountant to do the bookkeeping. Hire the expert to do the job so you can focus on your expertise.

I think the biggest misconception for business owners is that they think they have to know and do everything. So instead of relying on mentors and coaches, as well as other business owners through mastermind groups that work on solving problems and making life easier, they go it alone. Unfortunately, they have chosen a long, painful road. I believe that every business owner should have a mentor, a business advisor, or a business coach.

Wright

If you could offer only one piece of advice for creating and building a successful business, what would that be?

Abel

Down the road to business success, you'll have to answer questions and make decisions that you have never even considered. At some point, in order to get ahead, you might find yourself in a situation that begs you to compromise your values. Success—in life and in business—depends on how well you respond to such obstacles. Nobody ever said that starting and running a business was going to be easy. The truth is that sometimes it isn't even fun.

In the business world there are people who do things differently than they would under normal circumstances. It seems that in the pursuit of a buck, too many business builders are willing to sacrifice their values and their morals to speed things up and reach the pinnacle of success for which they have been working so diligently.

What kind of an existence did that make for you? Not a very satisfying one. Honesty, integrity, and reliability—these are all-important values. You don't make it to the top with these values intact by accident. Successful business developers never compromise their integrity or their values in the process of getting ahead. Your reliability, honesty, and character are key elements in your success as a person and a business builder. Have faith in the business process, in yourself, and in your vision.

Think positively at all times that things will work out for you and you will be successful. Growing a business is never an easy thing and success is not something that happens overnight. Be patient, be persistent, and maintain a positive attitude. Also, get coaching or other guidance when you need it.

Wright

So what does the future hold for Ed Abel? Do you have any plans, any goals to add to your success?

Abel

With the launch of Abel Business Institute, I'm branching out into many areas. I'm in the middle of growing my Mastermind groups and coaching practice by working with entrepreneurs and business owners. I'm also bringing on other business coaches to assist me in expanding our services to more areas. I've also developed the 12-step "Oops I'm In Business, Now What?" training workshops and modules. The name says it all, right?

Wright

Well what a great conversation, Ed. I really appreciate the time you've spent with me this afternoon to answer these questions. I've learned so much, especially the difference between an entrepreneur and a *Skillpreneur*. By the way, I want you to send me a copy of your "Ten Commandments for Business Success." I can use some guidance myself.

Abel

You've got it. You can also find them on my website at AbelBusinessInstitute.com.

Wright

Today we've been talking with Ed Abel, an iPEC-certified business coach. He's a trusted advisor and confidante to business owners who are serious about tackling tough and complex business issues and who welcome honest assessments and feedback about their business process and the decisions they make.

Ed, thank you so much for being with us today on *Roadmap for Success*.

Abel

You're welcome.

ABOUT ED ABEL

Ed Abel is an iPEC-certified business coach who turned a $5,000 loan into a 36 million dollar business. He is the creator and founder of Abel Business Institute, which offers proven business strategies and much needed support to small and mid-size businesses, owners, senior executives, managers and their teams, as well as corporations who want to take their business to a higher level.

Abel Business Institute assists those who are at a critical stage of their business. When the owner or manager of a business must evolve, grow, or otherwise change from a manager of things to a manager of people and finances—that's where they come in. Abel Business Institute takes you from being a *Skillpreneur*® who is essentially a technical expert, to a strategic thinker—a leader.

Ed created and leads the MBA Group, (Mastermind Business Alliance Group), that helps business owners achieve success in an environment where camaraderie exists, information flows, knowledge is shared, purpose is achieved, and everyone walks out more enlightened, committed, confident, and less alone than when they first arrived.

He is also the director of the business division at iPEC-Coaching School, training other coaches in his methods and philosophy. Ed created a series of seminar and training programs and modules called "Oops, I'm in Business, Now What?" He also talks to organizations and associations, sharing his insider wisdom about the ups and downs of owning your own business.

ED ABEL, Founder
ABEL Business Institute
352 7th Avenue Suite 605
New York, NY 10001
212.564.7584
www.AbelBusinessInstitute.com

ROADMAP *to* SUCCESS 5

DON MARUSKA

David Wright (Wright)

Today we are talking with Don Maruska. Everywhere we turn we face tough decisions. What's the best direction for our business? How can we resolve difficult problems in our community? Don Maruska has guided thousands of people to solve their most important issues. What's more, his process strengthens relationships so that the participants work together to implement their breakthrough solutions. Don speaks from experience as founder and CEO of three Silicon Valley companies. He has coached Fortune 500 companies, start-up businesses, and government leaders. He is author of the Amazon bestseller, *How Great Decisions Get Made: 10 Easy Steps for Reaching Agreement on Even the Toughest Issues.*

Don, welcome to *Roadmap to Success.*

Don Maruska (Maruska)

Thank you, David.

Wright

So what is the key to true success?

Maruska

The key to true success is understanding at a very deep level what we are truly hoping to accomplish. So often in life we operate at just a surface level. We think about what other people expect of us and compare ourselves with our neighbors or colleagues at work and fail to get in touch with what's truly important to us. In contrast, when we are clear about what we are hoping to accomplish and why it's important to us, we tap a deep source of positive creative energy. This approach enables us to develop outstanding solutions to difficult problems and successful implementation.

Wright

Why is reaching agreement on tough issues becoming so much more difficult? What can we do to overcome the obstacles?

Maruska

We're in a very interesting situation. With all of the advances in communication and communication technologies, we are like a spaceship hurtling through space. Unfortunately, our failure to discuss and resolve issues with one another threatens to blow the bolts off that technological spaceship. We see it in failed mergers and struggling businesses. We see it in countries around the world that are splitting up into small tribal groups. We see it in communities that can't reach agreement on what to do about schools, water resources, and other sensitive issues. All of these situations have become more and more difficult as people become more entrenched in their own views. Many people have become more interested in scoring points in their debates than they are in trying to discover what the truth is and solve issues together. We get to the situation where people hire attorneys as their designated "gladiators" and square off rather than square up with one another.

So, we have a critical need to tap the fundamental keys and critical tools that are necessary to have effective discussions that can bring real resolution to issues rather than further divisiveness.

Wright

Why do so many problems fester for so long without solutions?

Maruska

It's an interesting thing because we've got smart people. The question is why do smart people make dumb decisions or sometimes freeze and not make any decisions at all? The reason for this is that people don't address the real issue. They haven't identified the critical concern that stands in the way of successful resolution.

For example, a Fortune 500 company struggled to keep its hardware and software systems up to date. Leaders estimated that the firm was losing over a quarter of a billion dollars every year in inefficiencies and delayed product development. As an engineering-driven business, it had focused upon finding a technology solution. When we gathered leaders and line managers across its global operations, we uncovered a more fundamental problem and an easier and less expensive solution.

Before jumping to potential solutions, each participant took a few minutes to express his or her observations about the situation and the factors driving it. In order to ensure that everyone listened to one another, each participant reflected back on what the prior person said before offering additional comments. In the course of these insightful discussions, they identified a serious organizational disconnect between technology support services and the development groups. It wasn't that the technology providers lacked knowhow or resources; rather, they didn't have effective communication with the product developers about their needs. Consequently, they lacked information that would enable them to deliver efficient solutions.

With an effective diagnosis of the underlying problem, the team took organizational steps to better integrate operations. The solution proved to be a quicker and less expensive path than adding engineering resources.

This example highlights why it is so important to get to the real issue and make sure that we hear the wisdom each person has. So often in our culture there is a lot of talking but there is not much listening. There is even less appreciation for what is being said.

A good way to test our listening and confirm our understanding of others is to reflect back to them what we are hearing. This is a skill that is being lost in our culture as we shoot text messages and e-mails back and forth, but don't communicate thoroughly. This is especially true with people who have different points of view, different ways of expressing themselves, and difficulty really understanding one another's intent. We need to reflect back what we are hearing and communicate more closely.

Reflective listening is a powerful way to break through festering problems and discover the real issue. This is essential to move forward.

Wright

What are the key elements of the "Great Decisions Process"?

Maruska

The Great Decisions Process provides ten key steps to help people focus on their hopes, avoid the divisive dynamics of debate, and produce productive dynamics of dialogue and decision-making.

To highlight a few of them, the first one is to make sure we include all stakeholders. So often, decisions go awry or people get in opposition to one another because they don't have everyone in the discussion who needs to be involved. Our first step is to be sure to include them. People often avoid this because they are fearful of what some parties might say or worry that they have divergent interests. Rather than confronting their differences and understanding them, they try to avoid them; but avoiding them just causes the problems to become more severe. So, the very first step is engaging all stakeholders.

The second step guides participants to discover their shared hopes. I have found that even the most divided groups—the ones who have been at each other's throats, hired attorneys, spent money in opposition campaigns, or who have fought each other in the board room—have succeeded in identifying hopes that they share. When you ask people what their hopes are, why they are important to them, and delve deeper, participants discover a shared foundation for moving forward. When that happens, there is a huge sigh of relief that comes for all participants because they realize that they are in agreement about where they want to go. Then they can turn to a discussion about how to get there, and that's profoundly powerful.

The remaining steps continue with uncovering the real issue through the reflective listening I mentioned earlier.

Then, the Great Decisions Process provides steps to get all options on the table and have a discussion about them that is a one hundred percent exchange of information but no debate. The process focuses the discussion and brings it to closure by mapping solutions using the solution-finder technique that engages everyone to formulate solutions they can support together.

Wright

How do you translate hopes into action?

Maruska

While it's important to be clear about what you are hoping to accomplish and to be focused upon the critical issue, it's essential to have a process to translate those insights into options and results. That's where additional steps come into play to help participants stick with what they hope to accomplish and the creative mindset that they need to succeed together.

Modern brain scans show that when we are in a hopeful state we are tapping our very best mental capabilities. The parts of our brain, like the cerebral cortex and frontal lobes that can handle the most complex of issues, are the ones we engage when we are feeling hopeful.

In contrast, debates prompt fearful, self-protective thinking. The brain scans show us that fearful dynamics literally shut down our best thinking.

The real key becomes how to create a structure—a series of steps—to keep the hopeful, productive frame of mind in place so that we don't become derailed by our preprogrammed tendency to fall into debate and argument and into the fearful brain that is so destructive.

The concrete steps in the Great Decisions Process act like the software for our computers. Our computers are set up with certain default settings, just as people have a default tendency toward self-protection. If people don't have some other way of approaching challenging issues, they will become defensive and fearful. What we need is a human software program—a set of instructions to follow just like the computer follows a set of instructions with its software—that helps us stay in a productive frame of mind. Then we can articulate the issues, the options, the pros and cons of those options, get everything out on the table, and evaluate the information without the divisive debate that derails us.

Wright

What makes the Great Decisions Process effective?

Maruska

What makes the Great Decisions Process uniquely effective is how it sequences the steps. Think of it like a recipe for making a great cake. What's so critical in baking something is not having unique ingredients, although distinctive ingredients are important and there are many distinctive elements to the Great Decisions Process. What makes the recipe particularly powerful is how you put the ingredients together for great decision-making. People can follow this process in their businesses, they can follow it in their communities, and they can follow it in their homes.

Wright

What are the examples of how people have gained breakthrough results?

Maruska

Well, there are lots of examples. I have had the opportunity to work with thousands of people over fifteen years on this process. Let me give you a quick example.

There was the advanced research group for one of the top computer companies in the world that was looking to figure out what its next generation of products should be. They had assembled the best and the brightest people on the planet to work in this group. They quickly got into a debate about one person's point of view over another person's point of view. For three months they argued about what the software architecture or basic framework for their new products should be. They got no results at all, even after intensive effort. Management was having a tough time because these people were so talented, they couldn't just tell them, "Well, if you don't decide, we'll decide."

Many of these people could leave and go to any job in the world they wanted because they were really that talented. The dynamics got to such a bad point, however, that even the simplest issues became difficult. For example, they couldn't even agree on what color couch to have in their lounge. It was that frustrating for them.

We applied the Great Decisions Process, and they were able to agree on the platform for the next generation of products in one afternoon. They identified what they hoped to accomplish and discovered a basic alignment with one another. They got to the real issues about what they needed to resolve. They moved past the debate format into one where they had a productive discussion.

The key to this was that they got all the options out on the table. Each person offered an option he or she thought would be best in pursuing a desired architecture. Then they went through and had each person offer negatives about each of the options and positives about them. They went around first with the negatives on one option and heard a negative from each person. So everybody had a chance to say something they thought might be a shortcoming. Even people who might favor a particular option were invited and encouraged to identify what they might see as a shortcoming. In a similar way, they went around, one at a time, to state positives for the option.

When they did this for each option, everyone shared information without being either an advocate or an opponent. They moved out of the debate format and into the information exchange process. This telescoped what had been three months of fruitless debate into an hour's discussion of what were the negatives and positives of each of the options. They efficiently heard everyone's perspectives and reached a successful decision that enabled key development efforts for the future of the company to move forward.

This is an example of how a process can dramatically shift the dynamics in a group and provide a way for people to solve things that had been previously unsolvable for them.

Wright

The Great Decisions Process calls for one hundred percent information and zero percent debate. Why?

Maruska

When people debate, they protect information. They hide what they know are the shortcomings of their position from other people rather than revealing them. They aren't listening very effectively. They are really preparing their next point to defend their position or to attack somebody else. That's why focusing on exchanging information and having this structured way for people to express both the negatives and positives are very helpful.

We saw this also in a community that couldn't decide where to build a new school. It wasn't that they lacked resources—they couldn't agree on where to put the school and how to go about doing it. Through the Great Decisions Process, they discovered that their shared hopes were to provide educational quality, a fiscally responsible solution, and a location for a new school that wouldn't prompt undesired growth in their community.

When they looked at how each of the options addressed their hopes, and invited everyone to talk about the negatives and positives of each of the options (even though many participants had previously staked out positions on different approaches), it enabled them to free up their thinking. They came to a new and effective result that earned broad support. The school bond issue sailed through with over 70 percent of the vote—an extraordinary landslide. What's more, the community gained confidence that it could address tough issues together and reach positive outcomes.

Our culture has raised debate to a high art form, but it's a dead end. We need to move to an approach that promotes positive, constructive information processing and effective decision-making.

Wright

So, you can work through challenging situations without debate?

Maruska

Absolutely. For example, the president of a rapidly growing company wanted his employees more engaged in the company. He wasn't successful. We talked about how we could get people talking about what their hopes are for being in the business and why they are important to them, what issues they see and options to address them, and how they could evaluate those options. I recall the president worrying, "What happens if out of all this, they come up with a different direction than something that will work for me?" That basic fear had kept him from truly engaging his employees.

As thousands of others who have used the Great Decisions Process, the president discovered that they could come up with solutions that could work for everybody when they put their best thinking into practice and when they came at it from an approach of getting information on the table rather than debate.

He was delighted that they not only came up with a solution that worked for him but, in fact, his employees stepped up in a bigger way than they ever had before to help the president be more successful with the company. Furthermore, because they were concerned that he was working too hard and in an unsustainable way, they took on some of the president's tasks to balance his workload. So everybody won. That's what is possible when people have a great process for sorting through their difficult issues.

Wright

How can people learn the Great Decisions Process?

Maruska

The most effective way to learn the process is an approach that I discovered from the top surgeons in the world. I had an opportunity, in one of the companies that I started in the Silicon Valley, to work with such surgeons. They have a technique that they call "See One, Do One, Teach One."

A surgeon who wants to learn a new procedure scrubs up and joins the expert surgeon and observes what the surgeon does and helps out as he or she can in the process. That way the learner sees the reality of how the process works.

Next, the learner scrubs up and leads in the next surgery. The expert surgeon stands by to help out and give perspective on how that particular case and experience compares with others.

Then the next step in the process is that the learner has the job of going forward and teaching somebody else. In teaching somebody else, the learner ensures that he or she has learned the process in depth.

This "See One, Do One, Teach One" approach is the method we use to teach the Great Decisions Process. We do "See One," where someone who is experienced and successful in using the process leads a decision around something that is really valuable for the organization. So the organization gains the benefit of getting a great decision out of the process and seeing how to do the process. Then somebody from that work group picks up the next topic, but with an expert in the process present to coach him or her. Then the learner concretizes what was learned by teaching somebody else. This approach is the fastest and most cost effective way for people to learn because they get results right from the start as well as the capacity to apply the skills in subsequent situations.

Wright

As a business owner, can I guide the decision process when I have a stake in the issue or do I need someone from the outside to guide it?

Maruska

Well, that's a good question. It depends upon a couple of key factors. These are highlighted in a diagram in the book, *How Great Decisions Get Made,* that helps you sort through this question. Let me describe it and the key components.

There are two drivers that determine what talent you need to facilitate the process. The first is the importance of the issue—in other words, is there a lot at stake or not so much? The other key driver is what's the level of trust in the organization—is it high or is it low? For those situations where the issue is very important, there is a diversity of interests, and the trust levels are low, it benefits the participants to have somebody from the outside who is an expert in guiding the process to help them. It would be too much for someone with a stake in the issue to be both a participant and a facilitator.

It's a different situation if the level of trust is high and you've got somebody who has done the process and has been coached in how to do it. The person might be able to step up and handle a relatively important issue because the trust is there and he or she had some experience with which to guide the process.

Of course, if the trust level is high and the issue is not that critical, then it is something that a participant in the group can guide. I often recommend somebody who is not the boss because people frequently defer to the boss rather than give their best thinking. Also, if the boss is facilitating the process, he or she is less able to reflect on what others contribute.

So there are a variety of choices to consider. But the key is that it's better to use the Great Decisions Process, even if you don't have somebody else available, rather than fall back into old dynamics that we know are ineffective.

Wright

What a great conversation. I think I have learned a lot here. I've been taking copious notes. Everything you're talking about makes sense to me. I'm wondering why so many people don't do it already?

Maruska

That's a key question. Many people, even in the political world, ask me, "Well, gosh, this makes a lot of sense. Why aren't our politicians doing this?" or "Why aren't we doing this in our board rooms?"

One of the reasons is that our leaders have bought into the systems that got them there. For example, elected officials have risen because they have been good debaters. They are good at scoring points off each other. So, if we are going to change the process, we need the changes to come from the rank and file. We need people to say, "Hey, there is a different way we could be doing things. We need to change."

In fact, there is a great example about a woman named Sarah who was several levels down from a very autocratic CEO. She read my book and said, "I'd love to use this in my organization. How can I do it?" She became a positive force for change in her organization, not by controlling the CEO, but just by introducing the concepts in an informal way. For example, "Why don't we pull everybody together about this topic?" and "How about before we jump in, we hear from each of us about what we are hoping to accomplish around this topic and why it's important?" and "Since we haven't gotten clarity on this issue, how about if we reflect back to the last person who spoke before we offer our own idea about what might be at issue here?" and "Let's get different options on the table before we start discussing them."

As you can see, there is a conversational way to introduce the elements of the Great Decisions Process that enables people, even when they are not in charge, to help bring about change. Frankly, in this deeply divided world we live in, where our leaders are not bringing us together but more often than not are dividing us, we each need to pick up the mantle and move forward with the practical and effective things that we can do in our daily lives to make better decisions.

Wright

What great insight. Don. I really appreciate the time you have spent with me this afternoon, answering all of these questions. It's going to be very rewarding for our readers to find this information, especially the information about how they can learn more about the Great Decisions Process.

Today we have been talking with Don Maruska. He's guided thousands of people to solve the most important of issues in their lives, both personally and in business. What's more, his process strengthens relationships so that participants work together better to implement their breakthrough solutions.

Don, thank you so much for being with us today on *Roadmap to Success*.

Maruska

My pleasure, David.

About Don Maruska

Don Maruska guides Fortune 500 companies, growth businesses, government agencies, and communities to solve tough issues through a unique process of decision making. He draws from his wide ranging experience as vice president of marketing for the company that became E*Trade, as founder and CEO of three Silicon Valley companies (winning the National Innovators Award in 1988), and his work as a consultant, and as a Master Certified Coach. Don earned his BA from Harvard and an MBA and JD from Stanford University. He is the author of the Amazon bestseller, *How Great Decisions Get Made: 10 Easy Steps for Reaching Agreement on Even the Toughest Issues* (AMACOM 2004). Don has appeared on radio and television stations across America and is a frequent speaker and workshop leader.

Don Maruska
Don Maruska & Company, Inc.
895 Napa Avenue, Suite A-5
Morro Bay, CA 93442
805.772.4667
don@donmaruska.com
www.donmaruska.com

ROADMAP to SUCCESS 6

An interview with...

SANDRA FRITH

David Wright (Wright)

Today we're talking with Sandra A. Frith. Sandra is a licensed professional counselor, licensed marriage and family therapist, and holds a master's degree in Industrial Organizational Psychology. She is owner of Well Spring: Restore the Balance Counseling and Consulting Company, as well as the owner of Conscious Stream: Get in Touch with Your Own Natural Resources, a self renewal retreat company. She is a member of the Louisiana Counseling Association and a national member of the American Society of Training and Development. She has co-authored publications in the *Journal of Pharmacology and Experimental Therapeutics, Pharmacology Biochemistry and Behavior*. For training and development, she has written *Building Customer Relationships in Rural Hospitals with Employee Teamwork*. Sandra is a former contributing writer for the *Minute Magazine,* writing on topics of health, wellness, and community involvement. She has produced and directed weekend self-renewal retreats, she lectures on health and wellness topics at one of the local colleges, she is a corporate work-life balance consultant for companies throughout the United States and Canada.

Sandra, welcome to *Roadmap to Success.*

Sandra Frith (Frith)

Thank you very much.

Wright

So what is a work-life balance consultant?

Frith

A work-life balance consultant motivates employees to find what is important and what is not important at work and at home as well as looking at where their emotional energy is being drained. We look at what's causing the imbalance in their life. These issues so often blend over to each other—if something's not going right at home, it carries over to work, and if something's not going right at work, it carries over to home life.

Because we spend so much of our time in our work environment, the goal is to help people to find what it is that makes them feel fulfilled. This has a positive affect on the people around them. You can feel the "good vibrations" of a happy person. When you know that someone is truly happy in what they're doing at work and at home, they have a balance. Because we have so many things that can throw us off balance, a work/life consultant can help clients to recognize what needs to change. The goal is working well and living life.

Wright

So do you find that many companies struggle with employees who are out of sorts with their work life as well as their family life?

Frith

Yes they do. Actually, having one's work and home life out of balance costs companies billions of dollars. A work-life balance consultant can save on the high cost of turnovers and help cut costs of recruiting and retraining—it just makes a better work environment. You have more energy, more focus, and more commitment to what to you want to accomplish in your work-life. When employees recognize where their stressors lie and they learn what they can do about them, it is a win-win for everyone.

Wright

The title of this book is *Roadmap to Success* and your particular focus is "Help Wanted: Apply Within." How did this subject come about and how does it play a part in obtaining success?

Frith

The subject for this chapter came to me as I was driving one day. I was thinking about a client I am working with who is struggling over a work issue. He was not satisfied with his job. In addition, it was causing problems at home and marital issues. As I was thinking about my client, I saw a sign that said: Help Wanted: Apply Within. It just struck me that there are times in our lives where blaming someone else for our current life situation is easier than dealing with our own character flaws. But when you start looking at what is really going on and what you really need help with, it's all within you—your answers are within. My thought was that this applies to someone I was currently working with. The help he needed was to apply within to look at the part he was playing for his out-of-balance life.

Wright

That makes sense.

You speak about rediscovering a wellspring of understanding within. How does this help to make the journey of success clearer?

Frith

I believe when people discover that they have within themselves a divine intelligence as a guide, they can visualize what they want out of life, things become clearer and it's easier to map the course toward success for work/life balance.

Wright

In reference to "applying within," how do people know if they're getting a clear signal from their intuitiveness?

Frith

Once someone starts getting an intuitive insight as simple as to go back and check something that they might have left on the stove, they start the intuitive burst of insight. What really matters at this point is the action. Do you go back and check it or do you dismiss it? Just the very fact that you're actively listening provides a stronger message from within. Because intuition becomes stronger, it is a wellspring of understanding of what needs to be done. It gets stronger each time you pay attention to it—and your action is the key.

Wright

You mean I'm not the only one in the world who gets two blocks away from home and wonders whether or not I turned the iron off?

Frith

My grandfather told me, "If you can do something about it, you do it, and if you can't, you just can't." He was an inspiration to me and he taught me to value my intuition and to act on it.

Wright

Would you explain to our readers the technique you use to de-clutter your mind. What does CLEAR stand for?

Frith

CLEAR is an acronym for a technique I use with clients. There are a lot of negative thoughts that can go on and on in the client's mind. It can be everyday things that pop up, from the past or current events that can clutter the mind. It interferes with the quality of life and there is definitely no balance.

The CLEAR technique is used to assist clients with recognizing the clutter they are carrying around. I teach them to use the word "clear" as an acronym. We start out by using C words like *consciously* and *choose*, L words: *look* and *lessons*, E words: *evolving* and *energy*, A words: *acknowledge* and *accept*, and R words: *recognize, responsibility, release,* and *resistance.* When clients see that they are resisting, they are primed to release the thought that caused their stress. This begins the second step toward relief. We use the word clear backward: R for *receive*, A for *action*, E for *enthusiastic*, L for *lovingly*, and finally C for *creatively*. Clients learn to recognize that they have the responsibility within themselves to release the resistance and they will then experience relief. They are able to be more open to intuitive burst of insights that can be received actively, enthusiastically, lovingly, and creatively.

Wright

Do you think people are just too busy to enjoy a clear, uncluttered life?

Frith

I think so, but I think that once it is practiced, clients get more out of life. They start to pay more attention to what they are thinking about. It can be traced back to their thinking. They start realizing how much it matters in their life and they feel better both emotionally and physically. I believe that we take for granted practical tools that can give us more life. Just like breathing air, we take that for granted. My goal is to help clients pay attention to how they think and what they think about. When they practice this, they can start paying attention to their intuitive insights and at the same time improve work/life balance quality.

Wright

Tell us about your acronym, IGS.

Frith

I call that my "Internal Guidance System." It is the wellspring of the natural resource we all have within us. Your internal guidance system is your intuition, your wellspring—it is all of those.

Wright

Most of the books that I've read all down through the years say that women have much, much more intuitiveness than men. Why is that?

Frith

You know, I think that's true sometimes. But most of the time, I believe we are all able to tap into that resource. I think it is something that we just have to be encouraged to use, just as my grandfather encouraged me to use it.

Wright

Would you say that tapping into these natural resources within is the final destination on the road map to success?

Frith

No, it is not the final destination—it is an internal map to enabling you to move forward. There are many trips in life and I think that once you tap into your natural resource—that internal guidance system—you stay focused on what it is that you want to achieve toward a balanced life. When you start doing that, there is a tendency to achieve more success because you have learned the mapping skills. Your future destinations have greater successes and you'll know what it is that worked for you. You'll know what it is that you have to do to rely on your inner strength to pull yourself up by your bootstraps and keep going forward. Your action is required. Just pay attention and listen. The road map to success is recognizing the signs along the way—and you do that by going within to follow what your inner resource is telling you.

Wright

Many of authors say similar things about success and intuitive guidance, so how is what you're speaking about different?

Frith

Well, I thought of that many times and what I wanted to get across is that we all have different life lessons and we all learn differently. You never know what words are going to strike just the right balance and take on meaning for someone else. It gave me the motivation to work on the book project and to say what I felt the road map to success was. I believed that what I was saying might reach someone who needed to hear it; you just never know. I try as hard as I can to listen to what my inner resource is telling me to write for that special person.

Wright

What would you want potential travelers on the road to success to gain from your techniques?

Frith

What I'd like for them to recognize is their ability to go within and to visualize what it is that they want in their lives. If they are struggling with someone at work or at home, start looking within themselves for the answers. If they have any resistance, that is going to cause more and more grief. Once they let go of it, whatever it is, they're more open to receive the solution. The more they will see the successes that are in their life, the quality of their life will improve so much.

I am not saying that when they do this they are not going to have any problems at all in their life. What I am saying is that they will be able to move past obstacles—they will be able to move past things that seemed to be too great to move. But once they recognize that maybe they need to start looking at themselves instead of a co-worker or a spouse or a family member, I think that will allow them to have a clear picture of what a balanced work/lifestyle looks like. I would want readers to learn that it all starts from within; it is there and that is where their treasure to the road map to success is.

> *"Everything that irritates us about others can lead us*
> *to an understanding of ourselves"*—Carl Jung.

Wright

Well, what a great conversation. I've learned a lot here today. I have a lot to think about. I appreciate all of this time you've spent with us today answering all of these questions.

Frith

I enjoyed it very much, thanks for the opportunity.

Wright

Today we've been talking with Sandra A. Frith who is a licensed professional counselor and a licensed marriage and family therapist. Her focus in today's chapter is to outline steps for us to bring balance to our lives—all areas of our lives. Her hope is that our readers come to know that their road map is within themselves. Each of us has a wellspring as a natural resource to restore balance within ourselves and by starting the process, we get a clear path and we can map our way toward success.

Sandra, thank you so much for being with us today on *Roadmap to Success*.

Frith

Thank you.

About Sandra Frith

Sandra A. Frith is a Licensed Professional Counselor, Licensed Marriage and Family Therapist and hold a Master's Degree in Industrial/Organizational Psychology. She is owner of Wellspring: Restore the Balance Counseling and Consulting Company as well as the owner of Conscious Stream...*Get in Touch With Your Own Natural Resources*, a self-renewal retreat company.

She is a member of the Louisiana Counseling Association and a National member of the American Society of Training and Development. She has co-authored publications in the *Journal of Pharmacology & Experimental Therapeutics; Pharmacology, Biochemistry, and Behavior*; For Training and Development, she has written *Building Customer Relationships in Rural Hospitals with Employee Teamwork*. Sandra is a former contributing writer for *The Minute Magazine*. Her topics included information on health, wellness, and community involvement. She has produced and directed weekend self-renewal retreats, lectures on health and wellness topics at one of the local colleges, is a Corporate Work/Life Balance Consultant for companies throughout the United States and Canada.

Sandra Frith
1111 Homer Road
Minden, LA 71055
318.655.1259
restorethebalance@yahoo.com

ROADMAP to SUCCESS 7

An interview with ...

DR. KENNETH BLANCHARD

David E. Wright (Wright)

Few people have created a positive impact on the day-to-day management of people and companies more than Dr. Kenneth Blanchard. He is known around the world simply as Ken, a prominent, gregarious, sought-after author, speaker, and business consultant. Ken is universally characterized by friends, colleagues, and clients as one of the most insightful, powerful, and compassionate men in business today. Ken's impact as a writer is far-reaching. His phenomenal best-selling book, The One Minute Manager®, coauthored with Spencer Johnson, has sold more than thirteen million copies worldwide and has been translated into more than twenty-five languages. Ken is Chairman and "Chief Spiritual Officer" of the Ken Blanchard Companies. The organization's focus is to energize organizations around the world with customized training in bottom-line business strategies based on the simple, yet powerful principles inspired by Ken's best-selling books.

Dr. Blanchard, welcome to Roadmap to Success.

Dr. Ken Blanchard (Blanchard)

Well, it's nice to talk with you, David. It's good to be here.

Wright

I must tell you that preparing for your interview took quite a bit more time than usual. The scope of your life's work and your business, the Ken Blanchard Companies, would make for a dozen fascinating interviews.

Before we dive into the specifics of some of your projects and strategies, will you give our readers a brief synopsis of your life—how you came to be the Ken Blanchard we all know and respect?

Blanchard

Well, I'll tell you, David, I think life is what you do when you are planning on doing something else. I think that was John Lennon's line. I never intended to do what I have been doing. In fact, all my professors in college told me that I couldn't write. I wanted to do college work, which I did, and they said, "You had better be an administrator." So I decided I was going to be a Dean of Students. I got provisionally accepted into my master's degree program and then provisionally accepted at Cornell because I never could take any of those standardized tests.

I took the college boards four times and finally got 502 in English. I don't have a test-taking mind. I ended up in a university in Athens, Ohio, in 1966 as an Administrative Assistant to the Dean of the Business School. When I got there he said, "Ken, I want you to teach a course. I want all my deans to teach." I had never thought about teaching because they said I couldn't write, and teachers had to publish. He put me in the manager's department.

I've taken enough bad courses in my day and I wasn't going to teach one. I really prepared and had a wonderful time with the students. I was chosen as one of the top ten teachers on the campus coming out of the chute!

I just had a marvelous time. A colleague by the name of Paul Hersey was chairman of the Management Department. He wasn't very friendly to me initially because the Dean had led me to his department, but I heard he was a great teacher. He taught Organizational Behavior and Leadership. So I said, "Can I sit in on your course next semester?"

"Nobody audits my courses," he said. "If you want to take it for credit, you're welcome."

I couldn't believe it. I had a doctoral degree and he wanted me to take his course for credit—so I signed up.

The registrar didn't know what to do with me because I already had a doctorate, but I wrote the papers and took the course, and it was great.

In June 1967, Hersey came into my office and said, "Ken, I've been teaching in this field for ten years. I think I'm better than anybody, but I can't write. I'm a nervous wreck, and I'd love to write a textbook with somebody. Would you write one with me?"

I said, "We ought to be a great team. You can't write and I'm not supposed to be able to, so let's do it!"

Thus began this great career of writing and teaching. We wrote a textbook called Management of Organizational Behavior: Utilizing Human Resources. It came out in its eighth edition October 3, 2000, and the ninth edition was published September 3, 2007. It has sold more than any other textbook in that area over the years. It's been over forty years since that book first came out.

I quit my administrative job, became a professor, and ended up working my way up the ranks. I got a sabbatical leave and went to California for one year twenty-five years ago. I ended up meeting Spencer Johnson at a cocktail party. He wrote children's books—a wonderful series called Value Tales® for Kids. He also wrote The Value of Courage: The Story of Jackie Robinson and The Value of Believing In Yourself: The Story of Louis Pasteur.

My wife, Margie, met him first and said, "You guys ought to write a children's book for managers because they won't read anything else." That was my introduction to Spencer. So, The One Minute Manager was really a kid's book for big people. That is a long way from saying that my career was well planned.

Wright

Ken, what and/or who were your early influences in the areas of business, leadership, and success? In other words, who shaped you in your early years?

Blanchard

My father had a great impact on me. He was retired as an admiral in the Navy and had a wonderful philosophy. I remember when I was elected as president of the seventh grade, and I came home all pumped up. My father said, "Son, it's great that you're the president of the seventh grade, but now that you have that leadership position, don't ever use it." He said, "Great leaders are followed because people respect them and like them, not because they have power." That was a wonderful lesson for me early on. He was just a great model for me. I got a lot from him.

Then I had this wonderful opportunity in the mid-1980s to write a book with Norman Vincent Peale. He wrote The Power of Positive Thinking. I met him when he was eighty-six years old; we were asked to write a book on ethics together, The Power of Ethical Management: Integrity Pays, You Don't Have to Cheat to Win. It didn't matter what we were writing together; I learned so much from him. He just built from the positive things I learned from my mother.

My mother said that when I was born I laughed before I cried, I danced before I walked, and I smiled before I frowned. So that, as well as Norman Vincent Peale, really impacted me as I focused on what I could do to train leaders. How do you make them positive? How do you make them realize that it's not about them, it's about who they are serving? It's not about their position—it's about what they can do to help other people win.

So, I'd say my mother and father, then Norman Vincent Peale. All had a tremendous impact on me.

Wright

I can imagine. I read a summary of your undergraduate and graduate degrees. I assumed you studied Business Administration, marketing management, and related courses. Instead, at Cornell you studied Government and Philosophy. You received your master's from Colgate in Sociology and Counseling and your PhD from Cornell in Educational Administration and Leadership. Why did you choose this course of study? How has it affected your writing and consulting?

Blanchard

Well, again, it wasn't really well planned out. I originally went to Colgate to get a master's degree in Education because I was going to be a Dean of Students over men. I had been a Government major, and I was a Government major because it was the best department at Cornell in the Liberal Arts School. It was exciting. We would study what the people were doing at the league of governments. And then, the Philosophy Department was great. I just loved the philosophical arguments. I wasn't a great student in terms of getting grades, but I'm a total learner. I would sit there and listen, and I would really soak it in.

When I went over to Colgate and got into the education courses, they were awful. They were boring. The second week, I was sitting at the bar at the Colgate Inn saying, "I can't believe I've been here two years for this." This is just the way the Lord works: Sitting next to me in the bar was a young sociology professor who had just gotten his PhD at Illinois. He was staying at the Inn. I was moaning and groaning about what I was doing, and he said, "Why don't you come and major with me in sociology? It's really exciting."

"I can do that?" I asked.

He said, "Yes."

I knew they would probably let me do whatever I wanted the first week. Suddenly, I switched out of Education and went with Warren Ramshaw. He had a tremendous impact on me. He retired some years ago as the leading professor at Colgate in the Arts and Sciences, and got me interested in leadership and organizations. That's why I got a master's in Sociology.

The reason I went into educational administration and leadership? It was a doctoral program I could get into because I knew the guy heading up the program. He said, "The greatest thing about Cornell is that you will be in the School of Education. It's not very big, so you don't have to take many education courses, and you can take stuff all over the place."

There was a marvelous man by the name of Don McCarty who eventually became the Dean of the School of Education, Wisconsin. He had an impact on my life; but I was always just searching around.

My mission statement is: to be a loving teacher and example of simple truths that help myself and others to awaken the presence of God in our lives. The reason I mention "God" is that I believe the biggest addiction in the world is the human ego; but I'm really into simple truth. I used to tell people I was trying to get the B.S. out of the behavioral sciences.

Wright

I can't help but think, when you mentioned your father, that he just bottom-lined it for you about leadership.

Blanchard

Yes.

Wright

A man named Paul Myers, in Texas, years and years ago when I went to a conference down there, said, "David, if you think you're a leader and you look around, and no one is following you, you're just out for a walk."

Blanchard

Well, you'd get a kick out of this—I'm just reaching over to pick up a picture of Paul Myers on my desk. He's a good friend, and he's a part of our Center for FaithWalk Leadership where we're trying to challenge and equip people to lead like Jesus. It's non-profit. I tell people I'm not an evangelist because we've got enough trouble with the Christians we have. We don't need any more new ones. But, this is a picture of Paul on top of a mountain. Then there's another picture below that of him under the sea with stingrays. It says, "Attitude is everything. Whether you're on the top of the mountain or the bottom of the sea, true happiness is achieved by accepting God's promises, and by having a biblically positive frame of mind. Your attitude is everything." Isn't that something?

Wright

He's a fine, fine man. He helped me tremendously. In keeping with the theme of our book, Roadmap for Success, I wanted to get a sense from you about your own success journey. Many people know you best from The One Minute Manager books you coauthored with Spencer Johnson. Would you consider these books as a high water mark for you or have you defined success for yourself in different terms?

Blanchard

Well, you know, *The One Minute Manager* was an absurdly successful book so quickly that I found I couldn't take credit for it. That was when I really got on my own spiritual journey and started to try to find out what the real meaning of life and success was.

That's been a wonderful journey for me because I think, David, the problem with most people is they think their self-worth is a function of their performance plus the opinion of others. The minute you think that is what your self-worth is, every day your self-worth is up for grabs because your performance is going to fluctuate on a day-to-day basis. People are fickle. Their opinions are going to go up and down. You need to ground your self-worth in the unconditional love that God has ready for us, and that really grew out of the unbelievable success of The One Minute Manager.

When I started to realize where all that came from, that's how I got involved in this ministry that I mentioned. Paul Myers is a part of it. As I started to read the Bible, I realized that everything I've ever written about, or taught, Jesus did. You know, He did it with the twelve incompetent guys He "hired." The only guy with much education was Judas, and he was His only turnover problem.

Wright

Right.

Blanchard

This is a really interesting thing. What I see in people is not only do they think their self-worth is a function of their performance plus the opinion of others, but they measure their success on the amount of accumulation of wealth, on recognition, power, and status. I think those are nice success items. There's nothing wrong with those, as long as you don't define your life by that.

What I think you need to focus on rather than success is what Bob Buford, in his book Halftime, calls "significance"—moving from success to significance. I think the opposite of accumulation of wealth is generosity.

I wrote a book called The Generosity Factor with Truett Cathy, who is the founder of Chick-fil-A. He is one of the most generous men I've ever met in my life. I thought we needed to have a model of generosity. It's not only your treasure, but it's your time and talent. Truett and I added touch as a fourth one.

The opposite of recognition is service. I think you become an adult when you realize you're here to serve rather than to be served.

Finally, the opposite of power and status is loving relationships. Take Mother Teresa as an example—she couldn't have cared less about recognition, power, and status because she was focused on generosity, service, and loving relationships; but she got all of that earthly stuff. If you focus on the earthly, such as money, recognition, and power, you're never going to get to significance. But if you focus on significance, you'll be amazed at how much success can come your way.

Wright

I spoke with Truett Cathy recently and was impressed by what a down-to-earth, good man he seems to be. When you start talking about him closing his restaurants on Sunday, all of my friends—when they found out I had talked to him—said, "Boy, he must be a great Christian man, but he's rich." I told them, "Well, to put his faith into perspective, by closing on Sunday it costs him $500 million a year."

He lives his faith, doesn't he?

Blanchard

Absolutely, but he still outsells everybody else.

Wright

That's right.

Blanchard

According to their January 25, 2007, press release, Chick-fil-A was the nation's second-largest quick-service chicken restaurant chain in sales at that time. Its business performance marks the thirty-ninth consecutive year the chain has enjoyed a system-wide sales gain—a streak the company has sustained since opening its first chain restaurant in 1967.

Wright

The simplest market scheme, I told him, tripped me up. I walked by his first Chick-fil-A I had ever seen, and some girl came out with chicken stuck on toothpicks and handed me one; I just grabbed it and ate it; it's history from there on.

Blanchard

Yes, I think so. It's really special. It is so important that people understand generosity, service, and loving relationships because too many people are running around like a bunch of peacocks. You even see pastors who measure their success by how many are in their congregation; authors by how many books they have sold; businesspeople by what their profit margin is—how good sales are. The reality is, that's all well and good, but I think what you need to focus on is the other. I think if business did that more and we got Wall Street off our backs with all the short-term evaluation, we'd be a lot better off.

Wright

Absolutely. There seems to be a clear theme that winds through many of your books that has to do with success in business and organizations—how people are treated by management and how they feel about their value to a company. Is this an accurate observation? If so, can you elaborate on it?

Blanchard

Yes, it's a very accurate observation. See, I think the profit is the applause you get for taking care of your customers and creating a motivating environment for your people. Very often people think that business is only about the bottom line. But no, that happens to be the result of creating raving fan customers, which I've described with Sheldon Bowles in our book, Raving Fans. Customers want to brag about you, if you create an environment where people can be gung-ho and committed. You've got to take care of your customers and your people, and then your cash register is going to go ka-ching, and you can make some big bucks.

Wright

I noticed that your professional title with the Ken Blanchard Companies is somewhat unique—"Chairman and Chief Spiritual Officer." What does your title mean to you personally and to your company? How does it affect the books you choose to write?

Blanchard

I remember having lunch with Max DuPree one time. The legendary Chairman of Herman Miller, Max wrote a wonderful book called Leadership Is an Art.

"What's your job?" I asked him.

He said, "I basically work in the vision area."

"Well, what do you do?" I asked.

"I'm like a third-grade teacher," he replied. "I say our vision and values over, and over, and over again until people get it right, right, right."

I decided from that, I was going to become the Chief Spiritual Officer, which means I would be working in the vision, values, and energy part of our business. I ended up leaving a morning message every day for everybody in our company. We have twenty-eight international offices around the world.

I leave a voice mail every morning, and I do three things on that as Chief Spiritual Officer: One, people tell me who we need to pray for. Two, people tell me who we need to praise—our unsung heroes and people like that. And then three, I leave an inspirational morning message. I really am the cheerleader—the Energizer Bunny—in our company. I'm the reminder of why we're here and what we're trying to do.

We think that our business in the Ken Blanchard Companies is to help people lead at a higher level, and to help individuals and organizations. Our mission statement is to unleash the power and potential of people and organizations for the common good. So if we are going to do that, we've really got to believe in that.

I'm working on getting more Chief Spiritual Officers around the country. I think it's a great title and we should get more of them.

Wright

So those people for whom you pray, where do you get the names?

Blanchard

The people in the company tell me who needs help, whether it's a spouse who is sick or kids who are sick or if they are worried about something. We've got over five years of data about the power of prayer, which is pretty important.

One morning, my inspirational message was about my wife and five members of our company who walked sixty miles one weekend—twenty miles a day for three days—to raise money for breast cancer research.

It was amazing. I went down and waved them all in as they came. They had a ceremony; they had raised $7.6 million. There were over three thousand people walking. A lot of the walkers were dressed in pink—they were cancer victors—people who had overcome it. There were even men walking with pictures of their wives who had died from breast cancer. I thought it was incredible.

There wasn't one mention about it in the major San Diego papers. I said, "Isn't that just something." We have to be an island of positive influence because all you see in the paper today is about celebrities and their bad behavior. Here you have all these thousands of people out there walking and trying to make a difference, and nobody thinks it's news.

So every morning I pump people up about what life's about, about what's going on. That's what my Chief Spiritual Officer job is about.

Wright

I had the pleasure of reading one of your releases, *The Leadership Pill*.

Blanchard

Yes.

Wright

I must admit that my first thought was how short the book was. I wondered if I was going to get my money's worth, which by the way, I most certainly did. Many of your books are brief and based on a fictitious story. Most business books in the market today are hundreds of pages in length and are read almost like a textbook.

Will you talk a little bit about why you write these short books, and about the premise of The *Leadership Pill*?

Blanchard

I really developed my relationship with Spencer Johnson when we wrote The One Minute Manager. As you know, he wrote, Who Moved My Cheese, which was a phenomenal success. He wrote children's books and is quite a storyteller.

Jesus taught by parables, which were short stories.

My favorite books are Jonathan Livingston Seagull and The Little Prince. Og Mandino, author of seventeen books, was the greatest of them all.

I started writing parables because people can get into the story and learn the contents of the story, and they don't bring their judgmental hats into reading. You write a regular book and they'll say, "Well, where did you get the research?" They get into that judgmental side. Our books get them emotionally involved and they learn.

The Leadership Pill is a fun story about a pharmaceutical company that thinks they have discovered the secret to leadership, and they can put the ingredients in a pill. When they announce it, the country goes crazy because everybody knows we need more effective leaders. When they release it, it outsells Viagra.

The founders of the company start selling off stock and they call them Pillionaires. But along comes this guy who calls himself "the effective manager," and he challenges them to a no-pill challenge. If they identify two non-performing groups, he'll take on one and let somebody on the pill take another one, and he guarantees he will outperform that person by the end of the year. They agree, but of course they give him a drug test every week to make sure he's not sneaking pills on the side.

I wrote the book with Marc Muchnick, who is a young guy in his early thirties. We did a major study of what this interesting "Y" generation—the young people of today—want from leaders, and this is a secret blend that this effective manager uses. When you think about it, David, it is really powerful in terms of what people want from a leader.

Number one, they want integrity. A lot of people have talked about that in the past, but these young people will walk if they see people say one thing and do another. A lot of us walk to the bathroom and out into the halls to talk about it. But these people will quit. They don't want somebody to say something and not do it.

The second thing they want is a partnership relationship. They hate superior/subordinate. I mean, what awful terms those are. You know, the "head" of the department and the hired "hands"—you don't even give them a head. "What do I do? I'm in supervision. I see things a lot clearer than these stupid idiots." They want to be treated as partners; if they can get a financial partnership, great. If they can't, they really want a minimum of a psychological partnership where they can bring their brains to work and make decisions.

Then finally, they want affirmation. They not only want to be caught doing things right, but they want to be affirmed for who they are. They want to be known as individual people, not as numbers.

So those are the three ingredients that this effective manager uses. They are wonderful values when you think about them.

Rank-order values for any organization is number one, integrity. In our company we call it ethics. It is our number one value. The number two value is partnership. In our company we call it relationships. Number three is affirmation—being affirmed as a human being. I think that ties into relationships, too. They are wonderful values that can drive behavior in a great way.

Wright

I believe most people in today's business culture would agree that success in business has everything to do with successful leadership. In The Leadership Pill, you present a simple but profound premise; that leadership is not something you do to people; it's something you do with them. At face value, that seems incredibly obvious. But you must have found in your research and observations that leaders in today's culture do not get this. Would you speak to that issue?

Blanchard

Yes. I think what often happens in this is the human ego. There are too many leaders out there who are self-serving. They're not leaders who have service in mind. They think the sheep are there for the benefit of the shepherd. All the power, money, fame, and recognition move up the hierarchy. They forget that the real action in business is not up the hierarchy—it's in the one-to-one, moment-to-moment interactions that your frontline people have with your customers. It's how the phone is answered. It's how problems are dealt with and those kinds of things. If you don't think that you're doing leadership with them—rather, you're doing it to them—after a while they won't take care of your customers.

I was at a store once (not Nordstrom's, where I normally would go) and I thought of something I had to share with my wife, Margie. I asked the guy behind the counter in Men's Wear, "May I use your phone?"

He said, "No!"

"You're kidding me," I said. "I can always use the phone at Nordstrom's."

"Look, buddy," he said, "they won't let me use the phone here. Why should I let you use the phone?"

That is an example of leadership that's done to employees, not with them. People want a partnership. People want to be involved in a way that really makes a difference.

Wright

Dr. Blanchard, the time has flown by and there are so many more questions I'd like to ask you. In closing, would you mind sharing with our readers some thoughts on success? If you were mentoring a small group of men and women, and one of their central goals was to become successful, what kind of advice would you give them?

Blanchard

Well, I would first of all say, "What are you focused on?" If you are focused on success as being, as I said earlier, accumulation of money, recognition, power, or status, I think you've got the wrong target. What you need to really be focused on is how you can be generous in the use of your time and your talent and your treasure and touch. How can you serve people rather than be served? How can you develop caring, loving relationships with people? My sense is if you will focus on those things, success in the traditional sense will come to you. But if you go out and say, "Man, I'm going to make a fortune, and I'm going to do this," and have that kind of attitude, you might get some of those numbers. I think you become an adult, however, when you realize you are here to give rather than to get. You're here to serve, not to be served. I would just say to people, "Life is such a very special occasion. Don't miss it by aiming at a target that bypasses other people, because we're really here to serve each other."

Wright

Well, what an enlightening conversation, Dr. Blanchard. I really want you to know how much I appreciate all the time you've taken with me for this interview. I know that our readers will learn from this, and I really appreciate your being with us today.

Blanchard

Well, thank you so much, David. I really enjoyed my time with you. You've asked some great questions that made me think, and I hope my answers are helpful to other people because as I say, life is a special occasion.

Wright

Today we have been talking with Dr. Ken Blanchard. He is coauthor of the phenomenal best-selling book, *The One Minute Manager*. The fact that he's the Chief Spiritual Officer of his company should make us all think about how we are leading our companies and leading our families and leading anything, whether it is in church or civic organizations. I know I will.

Thank you so much, Dr. Blanchard, for being with us today.

Blanchard

Good to be with you, David.

ABOUT DR. KEN BLANCHARD

Few people have created more of a positive impact on the day-to-day management of people and companies than Dr. Kenneth Blanchard, who is known around the world simply as "Ken."

When Ken speaks, he speaks from the heart with warmth and humor. His unique gift is to speak to an audience and communicate with each individual as if they were alone and talking one-on-one. He is a polished storyteller with a knack for making the seemingly complex easy to understand.

Ken has been a guest on a number of national television programs, including Good Morning America and The Today Show. He has been featured in Time, People, U.S. News & World Report, and a host of other popular publications.

He earned his bachelor's degree in Government and Philosophy from Cornell University, his master's degree in Sociology and Counseling from Colgate University, and his PhD in Educational Administration and Leadership from Cornell University.

Dr. Ken Blanchard
The Ken Blanchard Companies
125 State Place
Escondido, California 92029
800.728.6000
Fax: 760.489.8407
www.kenblanchard.com

ROADMAP to SUCCESS **8**

An interview with...

BJ LEVY & AMORÁH ROSS

David Wright (Wright)

Today we're talking with BJ Levy and Amoráh Ross, successful professional coaches and co-owners of inviteCHANGE, a company created for those in search of meaningful processes that help catalyze learning and integrate a process for lasting change in one's personal and professional life. Their company's mission is to advance humanity and unleash the irrepressible human spirit.

Welcome to *Roadmap to Success*.

BJ Levy (Levy)

Thank you. I look forward to talking with you.

Amoráh Ross (Ross)

Thank you; I'm delighted to talk with you.

Wright

How does each of you define success?

Levy

Success to me is simple: waking up looking forward to each day, looking in the mirror and being happy with what I see, knowing I am making a difference in a way that is also energizing and fulfilling to me (so that I can keep doing it!), being on a growth curve, having sustained relationships, *and* making money while having fun doing what I love. My present definition is in sharp contrast to what was success to me when I was a lawyer, which was mostly about winning cases and making money. Enjoyment was not part of the equation.

Ross

During my career as a coach and instructor I've become known as "the acronym queen." I've found that creating acronyms is a challenging, fun, and easy way to stay aware of the many nuances that any particular word holds for me. As I think about success, it means **S**ustainable **U**nlimited **C**hoices **C**onsistent with **E**ssence in **S**ervice to **S**erenity.

Wright

You've each said that a process called Living Your Vision˚ has been a key factor in your success. What is this process?

Levy

Living Your Vision (LYV) is a process that exemplifies our transformative coaching paradigm, developing and deepening self-awareness on multiple levels, from knowing who one is at the core of one's being to making choices about what to do on a daily basis. It is a process for those who *want* and *are ready* to live a more intentional life in which they achieve more success (as they define success) and experience fulfillment in all areas of their life.

The LYV process will benefit anyone who is at a change point in life or who is looking for a deeper, more authentic life. The process is particularly helpful for people going through a relationship or job change or transitioning into another life phase (e.g., high school to college, first time in the work force, coming to mid-life), or for those in a personal or professional relationship who want to be more intentionally and consistently on "the same page."

Ross

Living Your Vision follows a simple and straightforward sequence based in the concept that "form follows thought." This sequence is Clarity, Alignment, Action, Results. In a group setting or one-on-one with trained facilitator-coaches, participants look inward to identify the unalterable truth about who they truly are, what values and beliefs are vital to their well-being, and take stock of what's working and what's not working in their lives. From this place of clarity, goals and desires are identified that align with who they are and their values and beliefs. Actions are then taken that move them toward those goals and desires. The results are reviewed every step of the way to ensure that those action steps are maintaining alignment with important values and beliefs, and that the individual is consistently choosing behaviors that fully express and expand one's clarity of who she or he is. You can see that the sequence continually circles back on itself, supporting an individual in living intentionally from the "inside-out."

Wright

I have an idea that the four elements of Clarity, Alignment, Action, and Results have specific meanings within the LYV process. What is clarity within this process?

Levy

The LYV process begins with gaining clarity about who an individual truly is at an "essence" level and experiencing the empowerment that such clarity brings. Many people expend unnecessary energy trying to be who they think others want them to be, never feeling quite comfortable in those shoes. They may even feel fraudulent and have thoughts such as, "If others only knew what I am really like inside . . ." (fill in the blank with any catastrophic impact you imagine.) When people step into the truth about who they really are and release all pretense, they free up energy to develop and experience a life filled with more meaning, enjoyment, and achievement.

Ross

By starting from the foundational clarity of "essence," an individual begins the process of reclaiming her or his original birthrights of the joy of being alive, the natural wonder and curiosity about life as an adventure, and freedom of self-expression. Each of these is a portal to boundless energy for everyday life and creates access points to truly inspired goals and desires. Daily living becomes an eager anticipation of what's next instead of merely a humdrum or hectic existence.

Levy

Some people believe that spending time on themselves is selfish and they carry in their mind a repeating script about the negativity of selfishness. These same people often wonder why they feel empty with nothing to give and feel put out when asked to do one more thing. The LYV process encourages an individual to spend quality time within to uncover and accept his or her "essence self" and then do what is important to feel fulfilled. Individuals can then be out in the world, giving from overflow, not from emptiness.

In addition to uncovering the truth of personal essence, the LYV process supports people in acknowledging their unique gifts. No two people have the same specific set of attributes, feelings, and ways of expressing. The expression of a unique journey brings deep satisfaction and may be exactly what someone else needs to hear to be inspired. An individual's willingness to know, speak, and act from essence gives permission for others to do the same.

Ross

Clarity also includes identifying key values and guiding principles that support and complement an individual's essence. While values and guiding principles are inherent in every human being, a combination of specific core values and principles are unique to each individual based on his or her life, family, and work experiences. Most decisions in everyday living are informed by these core values and principles and, through the LYV process, an individual forms the habit of consciously and deliberately assessing decisions and action steps through these lenses.

Levy

People live by personal mottos or guiding principles, whether consciously or unconsciously. The LYV process assists people to deepen their level of awareness of their own guiding principles and encourages evaluation to see which ones serve, which ones no longer serve, and which ones could be added in service to a higher quality of life. The process also encourages participants to word their guiding principles in a language that is most empowering.

Wright

After clarity, how does alignment fit in?

Levy

Alignment is the second major step of the LYV process, where people can think about and choose how they want to reach goals, what specific actions to take, and the priority and timeframes of those actions. It is similar to a strategic plan a business would make. While it is common business practice to strategize how to accomplish goals in furtherance of the business mission, individuals often don't do that in their personal lives.

Think how absurd it would be for an archer to start shooting arrows and then run into the field with a target to try to catch the arrows. Yet that is how many people operate—doing, doing, doing with no clarity about why they are taking action. They then wonder why they do not feel fulfilled. That would be a like an archer shooting more and more arrows and wondering why he is not hitting a target, when he or she doesn't know what or where the target is.

By strategizing and planning (aligning) what specific steps will support people being true to themselves, resulting actions create energy, meaning and purpose.

Ross

That's so true. Other processes that begin by crafting goals before gaining clarity and alignment put a bow and arrow in your hands and have you reacting from the ineffective sequence of fire, ready, aim. In the LYV process, it is only after gaining clarity about core essence and defining what values and guiding principles are truly important, that aim is purposely taken in the more effective sequence of ready, aim, fire: clarity to consistently behave from essence (ready), intentionally aligning on targets of meaning and importance (aim), and taking actions that reach the target (fire).

Levy

The LYV process encourages participants to ask themselves what they *really* want—not what they *should* want. By reaching into the desires of the heart, the individual's world opens up. What once seemed only a pipe-dream has the potential of manifesting when the energy of the heart's desire is part of the fuel for action. As

Harold Thurman Whitman has written, "Don't ask yourself what the world needs. Ask yourself what makes you come alive, and then go and do that. Because what the world needs is people who have come alive." The LYV process is a powerful tool for both coming and *staying* alive.

Ross

Another important aspect of alignment is to take the time to craft a plan that defines personal intentions behind what is really wanted, what is expected from life, and what the heart desires. For example, something I've identified I want is to be physically fit. However, when I think of it in those words, I consistently fail to exercise or go to the gym because it does not inspire desire within me. By stating what I want in the form of an intention, which is defined in the LYV process as a compelling statement of desire, I write it in my plan this way: I am strong and lean with stamina for anything I undertake. From this thought (remember the basic concept, "form follows thought") I regularly have the stamina to do whatever it takes to be strong and lean.

Levy

No two plans look alike and there is no wrong way to design a plan. The LYV process is designed to flexibly meet the specific needs and desires of individuals. A professional coach who is also a trained facilitator of this process, encourages individuals to be creative and "true to essence" in designing their life plans. One of our coach-facilitators often says, "This plan is a manual designed by you, about you, and for you." Just as an automobile manual contains instructions on how to reset the clock each spring and fall, a plan reminds people about their intentions, goals, and action steps. During a regular review process, people can see, acknowledge, and celebrate what they have already accomplished and be inspired by ideas they want to implement in the future.

Wright

It's abundantly clear how important alignment is. What about action?

Ross

For most of us, action may seem very straightforward since we each take millions of actions every day. However, in the LYV process, action is taken only after gaining clarity and defining alignment; this makes the action meaningful and intentional. In my experience from clarity and alignment, action becomes effortless—oftentimes organic. Instead of taking action for action's sake, action becomes purposeful movement toward a goal or desire that has been identified to bring fulfillment, satisfaction, or peace. Action that brings a heartfelt goal or desire into reality can actually add to an individual's well of personal energy instead of depleting it.

Levy

Coming from one's inner truth naturally inspires and empowers action. Coming from external "shoulds" brings about inner resistance and the need for extra effort to overcome the resistance. Because the LYV process is grounded in who a person is at his or her center, it accelerates the individual's ability to accomplish his or her most desired goals.

One of my life lessons is, "You always have energy for the next right step." If you don't feel energy for an action, it is either *not* the next right step or it is too big a step. It is important to break that larger step into smaller steps until you do feel energized.

An example for me was when I wanted to end a marriage of twenty years and leave my law practice of twenty-seven years (where I was in a law partnership with my husband!). Every time I thought about such a major transition, I would become overwhelmed and paralyzed. The LYV process encouraged and supported me to begin breaking down this huge life change into doable daily actions. Each step I took gave me energy and momentum for the next step, which would naturally appear. The result is that I kept my eye on my intentions, stayed true to my values, and now live the life I once only dreamed was possible.

Wright

That's an interesting perspective on action. Tell me please about the final portion of the sequence, results.

Levy

So often people, especially those who are hard-working and achievement-oriented, look at all there is on their to-do list and constantly feel overwhelmed. When they accomplish something, nothing more than a checkmark goes in place and they're on to the next thing on the list. By taking a few minutes on a regular basis to reflect on results (accomplishments, wins, achievements, and what has been learned), individuals can fill internal reservoirs of energy. The wins can be as small as, "I took time to breathe deeply every day," to something as momentous as, "My foundation was awarded $1 million to support women in the Congo." It is important to remember and honor what has been accomplished as well as look ahead to what there is remaining to do. When people acknowledge their achievements, they increase their confidence that they can achieve in the future while continuing to fill their internal reserves.

Ross

Another important aspect about results is for an individual to check in with how the process of achieving those results is being experienced. Asking questions like, "Has the journey to this point felt easy or difficult?" or, "Now that this result has been achieved, how does it align with my essence and values?" or even, "Now that this result has been achieved, is it something that I really wanted or does it occur as having been an unconscious 'should'?" By taking time to examine results, greater self-awareness is gained and course corrections can be made for next or future actions.

Levy

Yes, it is vital to routinely review and refine any plan. As people examine their results, they gain information for those refinements. One concept that encourages LYV participants to make a life plan is the freedom to change the plan. People are sometimes afraid to write a plan because they may not implement it all and then feel as though they have "failed." Knowing that the plan can evolve provides the freedom to experiment with new concepts. An individual can look at what is working (and do more of that) and what is not working (and do less of that or eliminate it altogether.) During routine review, individuals can see what they have already accomplished, be energized by that, and remember ideas not yet implemented and be inspired to implement them.

Wright

What do you believe is the primary component of the Living Your Vision process that makes it a powerful contributor to success?

Ross

The most important factor, in my experience, is that it provides a professional coach-facilitator as a steadfast partner and non-judging champion, consistently reminding people of the bigger picture of their life plan despite everyday snapshots that can obscure it. As life becomes realigned in accordance with a person's core essence, he or she pursues identified heart's desires using personal values and guiding principles as a yardstick. This supports taking empowered action steps and experiencing inspired actions as the coach helps the individual stay fully present within self and consciously intentional in daily actions.

Levy

By having a trained and experienced professional coach-facilitator in this powerful process, individuals gain new perspectives. They are able to reach higher and dive deeper because they don't have to "go it alone." They have a partner completely committed to them, their goals, their values, and their success.

Some people create a plan either on their own or in a class—and then nothing happens with the plan except that it becomes another dust-gatherer on a bookshelf. In the LYV process, the coach creates a safe environment for people to expand their horizons while staying true to what is important. The coaching relationship accelerates momentum while the individual develops self-sustaining habits.

Ross

Because the life plan is mapped out only *after* the client has gained clarity about core essence and values, Alignment is ensured through deliberate and intentional planning, goals are sourced from within according to what is truly desired, and action steps occur almost effortlessly because they're inspiring and exciting to take. Unlike most other types of planning, through the partnership of a coach, results will be checked against desired intentions, and incremental goal and action corrections will be made or a goal will be eliminated entirely if it's identified as a should.

Wright

What are the key principles of the Living Your Vision process that support success?

Ross

Our experiences over time since the LYV process was developed (in the mid-1980s) have shown that individuals effectively achieve conscious and sustainable success every day through the LYV facilitation followed by ongoing professional coaching partnership. There are several principles our professional coach-facilitators are trained to elicit. These have been described earlier: individual core essence, "form follows thought" and values/guiding principles identification. Other powerful models in the LYV process include Be-Do-Have, the CHOICES acronym, and Intention + Attention = Manifestation (IAM).

Levy

Our society is a "doing" society, with the expectation that if we keep doing more and more, we'll have enough "stuff," enough respect, enough love to be happy (or peaceful or fulfilled or whatever feelings or life experience is desired). The Be-Do-Have model in the LYV process turns this principle inside-out and asks what happiness (or peace or fulfillment) is for each individual, helping him or her explore how to begin with *being* happy (or peaceful or fulfilled) and recognize what sustains that feeling. The process provides empowering tools that help a person choose the activities, the people, and the way of behaving each day that supports the intentions identified in the life plan.

Ross

The CHOICES acronym is a key part of the life planning process. This acronym offers a reframing of thoughts or beliefs about how an individual can achieve her or his goals or desires. It stands for **C**hoosing **H**eart-centered **O**pportunities that are **I**nspiring, **C**ongruent, and **E**mpowering; **S**pecific and measurable actions follow. Too often resistance to planning can occur if an individual believes that once a goal is written, it is cast in stone and must be achieved or else. Many individuals have been freed to enjoy planning instead of dreading or avoiding it by replacing the concept of goals with choices.

Levy

Change is certain; how we deal with change is choice. Everyone faces difficult situations—often ones they would rather not face, yet the situations are there and the accompanying choices are there. The choice could be, "Do I hide or do I let others handle the matter?" "Do I get angry?" "Do I hope it will just go away or do I face the situation head on?" "Where is my personal power?" The LYV process encourages individuals to face change and challenges purposefully and intentionally. Participants learn they have real choice in their responses and discover new ways to consciously face recurring patterns. They gain insights that affect not only the particular situation, but all situations that have a similar theme.

Ross

Intention + Attention = Manifestation—the IAM model provides a simple yet powerfully effective way for an individual to remain focused on what's most important and to disregard anything that detracts from that focus. It further supports the concept that "form follows thought" so that the majority of what an individual focuses on is what has been identified as a true choice or desire. This focus increases the probability that any result is going to be the fulfillment of the individual's true choice or desire.

Levy

Intention is the experience a person truly wants underneath all expressions of "I want . . ." A common example may best explain the concept. A person will say she or he wants to lose ten pounds. When asked what losing the ten pounds will provide, the answer could be vitality, energy, or a better sense of self. It is the experience of vitality, energy, and a better sense of self the person really wants—that is his or her intention. By excavating the underlying desire, a world with more possibilities opens up. When people discover that what they really want is vitality and energy, weight loss becomes one means out of many. Action steps become easier because the lens of vitality and energy are more inspiring for making healthy choices in the moment than the idea of losing weight.

Attention is the energy an individual invests in his or her intention. If someone really wants the experience of vitality, and the choice is either to watch television or walk three miles, remembering the deeper intention often motivates the action of taking that walk. The vitality that naturally follows the walk begins to be self-motivating and the choice to walk again the next day becomes easier: "Of course I want to take the three-mile walk—I feel so much better after I do."

Manifestation is the result. Being unattached to how the manifestation appears is crucial. An individual may have started by intending to lose ten pounds. When he or she changes the intention to "I feel utmost vitality," the individual may actually lose five pounds or fifteen pounds—the number is not as important as the manifestation of vitality.

Wright

That's certainly a very clear Roadmap indeed. What are some of the obstacles that can be overcome as a result of applying the Living Your Vision process in daily living?

Levy

The LYV process is intended to be both inspiring on a large scale and supportive in day-to-day situations. One common scenario is facing a difficult conversation whether it is with an employee, a partner, or an elderly parent. By creating and looking at values and personal guiding principles for living, identifying and expressing core essence, and focusing on ultimate intentions, these self-developed guidelines provide a clear road map for handling any challenges. One person knows he or she wants to "speak their truth no matter what;" another is clear that "speaking with compassion" is a key principle to honor.

Another common and challenging opportunity where use of the LYV process makes a decided difference is when a person is no longer satisfied with his or her employment. The idea of changing jobs or shifting careers can be daunting, especially as one gets older. Yet the thought of staying in an unfulfilling job for ten or twenty or even more years may feel like one is in a death grip.

I have witnessed many people utilize the LYV process to become clear that leaving an old career is imperative. By identifying their underlying strong desire, achieving clarity, and embracing and setting strong intentions about making a smooth transition to a new career, individuals have implemented step-by-step plans that support their intentions. In doing so, these people have transitioned to new and much more fulfilling careers with greater ease than they previously thought was in the realm of possibility.

Ross

One client was a middle manager in an international commercial property development firm. He engaged in the LYV process in preparation to apply for a promotion to a position as director of a new branch office being opened in New York City. Through the clarity he gained about himself in the LYV process and over the course of our ongoing coaching, he increased his self-esteem, bolstered his confidence, and became viewed in his firm as the most obvious person to take responsibility for the success of this new branch. He has met and exceeded all expectations for the branch's contribution to the company's bottom line and remains consistently successful to this day.

Two amazing LYV experiences I've had have been with clients who began the LYV process as preparation for divorce. They each realized that it was vital for them to articulate the truth of their essence, identify their core values, create a purposeful plan, and be involved in a supportive coaching partnership as a precursor to taking that step.

One client became aware of the places in her relationship where she was unwilling or afraid to ask for what she wanted. Since she'd already made up her mind to divorce, she felt she had nothing to lose by speaking up as she went through LYV. As she spoke up, she found her husband to be open and responsive and he began speaking up too. Her surprising success was that they actually ended up recreating their marriage on a different basis of relating to one another instead of divorcing.

Another client was able to stay calm, at peace, and clear-headed as she went through a very trying divorce. She steadfastly remained focused on her values and what she wanted, while her soon-to-be-ex-spouse tried to hide assets, avoided critical financial discussions, and become a new father with his mistress. After the dust had settled, her ex-husband expressed admiration for her rock-solid presence throughout the divorce. Her success was that she stayed true to her values and received every asset in the settlement that was most important to her.

Wright

Give an example, please, about how the LYV process has contributed to your personal success.

Levy

Using the LYV process, I transitioned from my long-time career as an attorney to become a personal and professional coach. For many of the twenty-seven years I was a lawyer, I had thought about changing careers and each time, the enormity of the change was paralyzing. Through the LYV process and in partnership with my coach, I became clear that a change was long overdue. When my coach asked, "When is your last day?" a question I had been avoiding asking myself, I set the intention to be out of my law office in six months. I was energetically freed to start making a specific plan of action. The result was that what for years had seemed impossible started to become a reality—one that I created out of intention and actions aligned with my values. I was out of my law office on the exact date I had set six months before. After following this process for myself, I knew that anything was possible, both for me and for anyone who would commit to the process.

I review my own LYV plan regularly and I am energized by all that I have accomplished and reminded about the ideas I had forgotten. By checking in, I stay "current" with myself and make the small and large shifts with greater ease. More importantly, *how* I live day by day is dramatically different than how I lived when I was a lawyer. I feel calmer *and* fulfilled. People who knew me when I was a lawyer tell me how much happier I appear (and they are right!).

Ross

When I was about ten years old, I had an experience swimming in a lake that created within me a strong fear of being in a body of water. When I went through the LYV process in 1997, one of the intentions in my life plan was, "I joyously and fearlessly play in oceans, rivers, and lakes." As I wrote that intention, I knew only that I wanted to once again experience the freedom and comfort I'd felt while swimming before the fear was born. I had no idea what choices or action steps would get me there.

About three weeks after writing my intention, I received an invitation to participate in a retreat in Hawaii and swim with the wild dolphins in the ocean. I recognized this as a choice I could make toward fulfilling my intention and I set about planning and taking the action steps necessary to manifest it—saving the money for the trip, learning about Hawaii, the ocean, and dolphins, etc. My coach supported me over the eight months between accepting the invitation and arriving in Hawaii for the retreat. He asked powerful questions, helped me explore my fear through inquiry questions, and steadfastly believed in my ability to fulfill my intention and reclaim my ability to enjoy swimming again.

The retreat was all I had hoped it would be and more. My desire to swim with the dolphins outweighed my fear and by the end of the two weeks, I was once again comfortable and joyful in the water. Not only did I shift my fear, but during the next ten years I led retreats to Hawaii and helped others overcome their fears of the water too.

Even though I did the LYV process many years ago, my LYV plan is still alive and at work for me. Every year on New Year's Day, I review the entire plan and set new intentions. From that review process I then make a poster that visually depicts the theme I've identified for the New Year. I keep it next to my desk throughout the year as a reminder of what's important for me to accomplish by the next New Year's Eve. Then the cycle begins anew. Because LYV is such an integral part of my daily living, I stay focused on what I want, experience joy in living, and achieve success within my own definition.

Wright

As professional coaches and instructors of professional coaches, it's obvious that each of you is passionate about coaching as a contributor to success. What do you believe is the reason for that?

Ross

In June 2006 a *Washington Post* article by Shankar Vedantam spotlighted a growing trend of social isolation due to a decline of social ties in the United States. As documented in a General Social Survey, funded by the National Science Foundation, "A quarter of Americans say they have no one with whom they can discuss personal troubles, more than double the number who were similarly isolated in 1985 ... The comprehensive new study paints a sobering picture of an increasingly fragmented America, where intimate social ties—once seen as an integral part of daily life and associated with a host of psychological and civic benefits—are shrinking or nonexistent."

Partnering with a professional coach can reduce social isolation merely by adding one more meaningful relationship to your life. In addition to that, by engaging in a relationship in which you are encouraged to focus on your essence, your values, and your desires, you're more available and better equipped to create and sustain other supportive social ties with family, friends, and colleagues.

Most of the people I meet, whether students or clients, want to have a deeper connection with others and to make a difference in the world. Through coaching, that can occur more quickly and effectively than going it alone.

Levy

Coaching is an opportunity to maximize your support. A coach is a person who will listen and ask questions to uncover your wisdom and true desires. A coach is someone you tell anything without fear of being judged. A coach sees you as whole, capable, resourceful, and creative rather than someone who needs "fixing." A coaching relationship helps you keep current in your own life, check in on what is most important, and discover your own answers—answers that move you in the direction you want to go.

Wright

What message do you wish people to hear so that they can learn from your success?

Levy

In a recent book, *Change or Die: the Three Keys to Change at Work and in Life*[1] author Alan Deutschman found that the key to helping people get unstuck is an emotional relationship with a person or with a group who inspires you to have the confidence to say, "If you can do it, I can do it." That is what professional coaching and the LYV process provides: tools, inspiration, and an emotional relationship with a supportive coach who focuses only on your ability to live your highest expression of essence every day.

There are many examples of people whose lives have been forever altered as a result of participating in the LYV process. I have worked with countless clients who feel "stuck" in a job, and paralyzed about taking any forward steps. When they get in touch with the truth of who they are, hear about others like them who have made the great leap, and learn to trust the process themselves, they start to see the possibility of another way. Once one possibility opens up, the dam is broken for a myriad of other choices. Once choice is available, energy is released to begin to explore and develop possibilities.

Being a support for others to find their fulfillment from my authenticity is success for me.

Ross

The point at which I began to feel truly successful was when I stepped into my personal definition of success and started living my life in alignment with my essence and my values, defining my intentions and choices from the inside-out. The LYV process and my amazing professional coaches over the years have played a big part in bringing me to that point. By releasing the need or belief that success looks only a certain way as defined by society, family, or any other means, individual expression is unleashed. Instead of being a series of dusty rest stops on the way to its end, life becomes an intriguing and exciting journey.

I invite you to define success your way—and I dare you to live your life unleashed!

About BJ & Amoráh

After twenty-seven years of practicing law, BJ chose to transform her life to one of joy, play, satisfaction, and meaningful contribution. She brings the experience of her personal transformative journey, her innate wisdom, and refreshing spirit to all she does—instructing a class, motivational speaking, and coaching relationships. Founder of the Institute for Voice Dialogue Coaching, BJ brings special expertise in assisting clients to acknowledge and use the multiple "selves" to shift from automatic reactions to empowered, creative choices. A long time senior faculty member of inviteCHANGE, BJ is now one of its co-owners.

As one of the first coaches in the world and certified in 1999 by the International Coach Federation, Amoráh built her successful coaching career primarily as a life coach working with individuals and groups interested in self-empowerment and successful life balance. Amoráh is co-owner of inviteCHANGE and Director of Training. Her unwavering commitment includes mentoring emerging coaches and she volunteers as an ICF Credentialing Assessor.

Amoráh's passionate commitment is to provide curriculum and services that continually raise the bar for coaches worldwide. This fuels inviteCHANGE's mission to incorporate the transformative living paradigm into all human relationships.

BJ Levy, PCC and Amoráh Ross, MCC
inviteCHANGE and Living Your Vision®
110 W. Dayton Street, Suite 202
Edmonds, WA 98020
Phone: 425.778.3505 or 877.228.2622
www.invitechange.com

Living Your Vision® is a proprietary process exclusively owned by and licensed through inviteCHANGE.

ROADMAP to SUCCESS 9

An interview with ...

GWEN DAWSON

David Wright (Wright)

Today we're talking with Gwen Dawson. Gwen was born in Scotland, grew up in Jamaica, and then moved to Nevis. After teaching mathematics and physics for seven years in the Eastern Caribbean, she opened her own tutoring business on the beautiful island of Saba. She has observed the effect of her students' thoughts on their self-esteem and productivity. She asserts that success has more to do with confidence than abilities. She recommends a variety of techniques that she has found helpful, including meditation, energy therapies, and breathing techniques and she guides others in expanding their awareness so that they notice and bring into their lives what will produce success.

Gwen, welcome to *Roadmap to Success*.

What is "presence"?

Gwen Dawson (Dawson)

I will refer to "presence" as consciously placing our attention where we choose. We automatically place our attention on breathtaking experiences like a beautiful flower, amazing music, or a wonderful aroma. A child who is totally absorbed by a television program may not notice someone passing between him (or her) and the television. We say we are "immersed in," "gripped by," and "wrapped up in" "captivating" and "alluring" experiences. It is our attention that these experiences hold onto.

Being mesmerized by the scent of roses can be a great pleasure. We may decide instead to hear the words of the loved one standing beside us. Our ability to choose where we place our attention can be used to improve our quality of life.

Wright

How can presence benefit us?

Dawson

Bringing more awareness into our lives creates a stillness of the mind that heightens our skills of observation. This tunes us in to the desires of our hearts or what success means to us and helps us to notice what affects our success. We can then more easily make decisions that are aligned with our wishes. Through these choices we create happier lives with more fulfilling relationships and careers.

Wright

Is presence a type of prayer or meditation?

Dawson

Prayer is one way in which we can achieve presence. I feel true prayer is placing our hearts on the altar of God—feeling a magnificent power before which we wish to bow in reverence. Through the presence of mind and openheartedness of prayer we expose our innermost thoughts and feelings to ourselves. We see our fears, our wishes, and the purity of our motives. Seeing the truth and the beauty of our own hearts builds our trust in ourselves. As we get to know ourselves and God within us, we open ourselves up to understanding and wisdom.

Placing our attention with complete acceptance on our thoughts is a transforming meditation. By paying attention, we notice the topics of our thoughts. Our thoughts are the sources of our feelings. As we observe them with acceptance, we quiet our minds and develop the freedom to create pleasant thoughts.

Focusing on the breath is another powerful meditation technique. It helps us to relax, release negative energy or emotions, and breathe deeper, inhaling more oxygen and more energy. The breath and the mind work together to direct energy for healing. I found meditating on bringing energy into the chakras, one at a time from base to crown, a fast way of improving my mood. "Emotional Freedom Techniques" seem to go beyond this and heal the underlying blockages to positive emotions.

Investing time and attention in enjoying tastes, smells, sounds, sights, and sensations, we experience other powerful relaxing meditations. Many activities such as dancing, singing, eating, listening to music, and swimming are considered meditations by participants who become completely focused on the present moment. The more we place our attention on activities we enjoy, the more we allow them to bring us joy, relaxation, and energy.

Wright

How have you used presence in your life?

Dawson

When I first considered the contract for writing a chapter in *Roadmap to Success,* I was gripped by the fear of being cheated. I felt overwhelmed by distrust and would have given in to the confusion I felt if I had not had the presence of mind to recognize it for what it was—fear built from things in my past.

After some assistance from meditation and Emotional Freedom Techniques to dissipate the overwhelming emotions, I had enough clarity on the situation that I was able to reword my questions to be received by someone who was being open and honest with me, willing to hear my wishes, treat me fairly, and decide upon a win-win agreement for us both.

Neuro-linguistic Programming also provides useful methods for freeing ourselves from the patterns we created through our interpretations of the past.

Wright

Presence seems very helpful in relationships.

Dawson

Yes, it helps us to create a positive outlook on life so that we are more pleasant to be around. By opening our hearts, we allow ourselves to feel the love of others. We are more likely to be patient and understanding, especially with children. Our thoughts are more positive, so we more easily see the good in others and disregard tiny inconveniences like children spilling things, printers running out of ink, or clients arriving late.

A clearer view of reality makes it easier for us to describe what we are feeling and why. We take responsibility for our emotions and actions and see them as the responses we choose out of many possible responses to each situation. We act out of our desire to find solutions, to understand and to create positive experiences. We aim to resolve misunderstandings immediately in compassionate, effective discussions.

When we allow children to shoulder their own responsibilities, we have more energy to enjoy life. This begins with expecting children to be part of the team to help keep the house pleasant for all who share it. Having young children do little things such as pushing in their chairs or putting their toys back in the box after playing, gets them accustomed to cleaning up after themselves. Rules, responsibilities, and consequences must be clear and adhered to in order to be respected. The only way to stop a child from throwing tantrums is to show the child that you will not change your mind because of a tantrum. The same principle works for adults!

Respecting and guiding children helps them to learn how to communicate with respect. When we show them that we enjoy making them things they like or taking them to places they enjoy, they feel special. Asking them to do things for us and showing our appreciation gives them opportunities to feel the joy of giving and make it a part of their lives.

Presence encourages us to welcome opportunities for growth and forgiveness as we recognize the freedom and positive emotions they create. The ASHE group from Jamaica has a technique that helped me to forgive someone I thought I had already forgiven. I wrote a letter to the person, stating exactly what had happened and the emotions I had felt in response to these events. Then, I found good things that came out of the events and thanked the person for those things. Of course the letter does not have to be sent. It is for our own benefit.

Wright

How can presence help us to be successful?

Dawson

If you love the risks and challenges of buying and selling houses, then it will excite you. You will feel driven to enjoy this adventure. Your goals may have to do with profits and the beautiful transformations you wish to create. You will feel successful attaining these goals.

In order to be successful we must have goals we desire to accomplish. Then we must have the things we require to achieve our goals. Being comfortable, appreciated by others, and having beautiful surroundings are some of the extras that make being successful easier and more enjoyable. More importantly, we must feel our ability to be successful. This confidence can be developed by specific choices in the areas that affect our self-esteem.

We more easily create positive thoughts about our ability to succeed when we feel refreshed. A walk after dinner or some other type of exercise may help you to sleep well. Our bodies heal and maintain themselves better when we relax. We can meditate, read a good book, stretch, enjoy nature, or listen to music to relax. Warm socks sometimes make an incredible difference to my sleep. Making your bedroom a pleasant, inviting space with fresh air, nice clean sheets, or some white noise to muffle sounds from outside may help. Eating a few hours before going to bed and avoiding naps are also recommended. Deep breathing in fresh, clean air can be more refreshing than a nap.

Imagine waking up feeling refreshed, carefully and lovingly shaving, washing, drying, and applying lotion or aftershave to your amazingly intelligent, beautiful body. As you dress, recall that your clothes are made of colors that suit your complexion, tailored to fit your figure perfectly and to accentuate your best features. Look down at your feet and see your nicely polished shoes or beautiful toenails. Just putting on clothes we feel good in is very uplifting. We are therefore more likely to do well in an interview, to be more convincing in a negotiation, or to feel the confidence to approach someone to make friends.

Clothes can make us feel better about how we look, but at some time we will probably take them off. Changing your weight or toning your muscles may be a greater boost to your self-esteem. If we choose exercise we enjoy doing, start with an easy target, and gradually increase our goal, we are more likely to stick to it so that we benefit from it long-term. Exercise makes us feel energized, more alert, and stronger. It strengthens many things including the heart, bones, and lungs and cleanses the body through perspiration.

We usually work best when we take breaks, even just for five minutes about every thirty minutes. Taking a break is better for our eyes if we are behind a computer screen or working on something with our hands. It is good for our mood for many reasons. We feel more alert and relaxed. We feel good about ourselves for choosing to quickly and easily increase our productivity and accuracy in the best interest of ourselves and our employer. Getting a glass of water is a good excuse for a break. Water cleanses our bodies of both physical waste and negative energy and affects our mood and health in many positive ways.

When we listen to our bodies they tell us what the experts say—to adjust our furniture to make our bodies comfortable and to get up and stretch. They also guide us in our food choices. Food affects our emotions as well as our energy and health. Fresh fruits and vegetables tend to make us feel more alive than other types of food. Sometimes our bodies are asking for certain nutrients through our cravings. When we notice what tastes we like, how we feel after different food, and what food we enjoy, we can more easily give our bodies the best fuel.

The more we pay attention to our mind, the more we understand how it works. When we attempt to remember something, it is like sending a little man to retrieve that memory. Once we take our mind off it he can go and find the memory. Trying to remember is like calling him back to send him again. When we give ourselves time to sleep on a problem, we benefit from natural abilities of the mind that are at least partly subconscious.

Have you ever tried to concentrate and found that your mind kept wandering off to something else? Our memory, alertness, and ability to concentrate can be affected by worry. Once we have figured out what we were worrying about, we can find solutions or use affirmations or other methods to alter our thought patterns. It may be something as simple as having to remember to feed the cat. Once we do it or write a note that we are sure to see, we can reclaim the mental energy we were giving to constantly reminding ourselves. If it is something that is not this easy to solve, we can decide to create a positive thought each time the worry comes up. Focusing on what you would like to happen, instead of what you dislike, is said to create your wishes. Even if it does not, it feels much better.

When we allow ourselves to feel the negative emotions that stole our desire to live, release them and forgive ourselves and others, we reclaim our joy and our lightness of heart. Do you recall feeling unwell and then taking your mind off that feeling to do something you enjoy and noticing afterward that you felt much better? There are people who claim they have healed themselves of cancer just by laughing. Happiness definitely has a huge positive influence on health. When we place our thoughts on positive reasons to live, we find joy and the drive to go on.

Once we feel good about how we look and feel in our bodies and have developed presence of mind, we can focus on conversations, reading, building relationships, and on our careers. We all have things that are important to us—things we like to talk about and information we find interesting. When we make the time to inform ourselves about these things, we feel more intelligent and confident in conversations.

We can also pay attention to the quality of our conversations. Are they uplifting, encouraging or rejuvenating? R. Neville Johnston's book, *The Language Codes,* is of great value in creating more conscious empowering language. We feel better when we find positive things to discuss, whatever the topic.

Wright

What are some ways to increase our energy?

Dawson

We are more likely to feel happy through minor inconveniences after a restful night's sleep, an enjoyable, healthy breakfast, and a pleasant morning at the office. We feel more confident and have more energy to give, so we can have a more positive influence wherever we are. Certain things give us energy, other things take it away. Many of these things we share, others differ from person to person. Showers or baths seem to improve everyone's mood, but the type of music I like may not be pleasant to any fifteen-year-old. One of the main purposes of presence is to guide us in discerning what we like.

The things that give us energy are usually those we enjoy doing. What makes you laugh? Do you love nature? Who do you love? What do you love to do? What makes you feel loved? Love is the very foundation of society—the reason for the continuation of the human race. When we feel love we are raising our energy. We can do this by experiencing beauty, a fresh red rose, the character of a person we describe as an angel, or sounds that make us feel alive and happy like music, birds, or the sea. We feel love when we enjoy touching or playing with pets, children, and friends. Our bodies and our universe were designed to bring us enjoyment. Allow yourself to enjoy!

Wright

How do we free ourselves from society's norms?

Dawson

The biggest step is noticing that norms exist and deciding to choose our own experiences instead of blindly fitting in. There is no reason for us to build our expectations for our lives on patterns we have perceived in others. We can learn from the mistakes of others and show others that it is okay to be happy, healthy, and wealthy. We are designed to live so that we feel good about ourselves and enjoy life. The book and movie titled *The Secret* give the powerful technique, used by Beethoven, Shakespeare, Einstein, and others to make their wishes come true.

Society has placed the character of the martyr on a pedestal. Would you like anyone to suffer for you? Those who love you do not wish for you to suffer. They wish for you to be happy, healthy, and successful.

What is your image of a successful person? Does your heart tell you to love, to enjoy life, to trust, to forgive, and to look after yourself? It is time for us to enjoy life, to notice the rubbish we used to believe, and to laugh at it as we throw it away—far away. It is time for us to create beautiful loving relationships, to see the beauty in each other, and to trust that deep down we all desire what is best for each other.

Wright

How do we create successful teams?

Dawson

The happiness, presence of mind, and confidence that make individuals successful also make teams successful. A team's enjoyment of working together can create the drive to go to work, even if the job is an unpleasant one. By expressing confidence in each other people can encourage their teammates to succeed in more challenging tasks.

Happy people are more pleasant to work with and more productive. They uplift their team and set the other members at ease, improving the atmosphere and drive to succeed.

Presence enables us to see opportunities to help others to feel more confident such as complementing them on a job well done or clothes we admire. Letting them know that their input, intelligence, skills, and time are valued empowers them. Feeling appreciated at work, they are more inclined to make sensible decisions instead of acting out of the fear of being fired or getting in trouble. Feeling valuable also motivates them to take better care of themselves and to be willing to put in some extra effort for their employer.

Asking your employees what would make their work easier or more pleasant can make them feel appreciated. Something as simple as pens that work better or new keyboards may make a big difference. Perhaps you could provide snacks, coffee, tea, and a refrigerator—whatever is feasible and affordable to make the lives of your employees more pleasant.

Often it may take a tiny gesture to make someone feel valued, such as asking the janitorial staff what their ideas are on improving how the office looks. They may have a big influence on how the day goes if they are the first people everyone sees as they enter the office or if one of them must be approached to obtain a cup of coffee. You could let your team pick out plants for the office or suggest colors to paint the walls. Even if you choose to do otherwise, asking for the opinions of your employees makes them feel heard, especially if you give them the reasons for your decisions.

If you are the team leader, talking with your team members with respect and genuine care for their wellbeing can make a big difference. They may feel afraid of you since their job is in your hands. You can show your trust in them by giving them the benefit of the doubt if they call in sick occasionally, or better still, encouraging them to enjoy time off work while they are well. Encouraging your team to take breaks, have fun, and do other things that make them feel good about themselves could be very good for your productivity and the atmosphere in the office. They will feel good about working for you, which will make their job more valuable to them. They will therefore be willing to do more for you because they appreciate the way you treat them.

Whether it is a family, a sports team, or the workers in an office, each person must respect the other members of the team in order to maintain peace and the team spirit.

The best way to teach this is by example and gently but firmly holding others to this standard.

Wright

How can we do work in a playful environment?

Dawson

A playful environment is a natural recipe for happiness and success. Success comes from enjoying what you do. Children learn best when they are relaxed and having fun. It is natural to assume that when work becomes play we accomplish more and feel better doing it. Human beings have a genuine desire to create success in their lives. Creative forces flow when we feel lighthearted, comfortable, and happy. It is possible to come up with life-changing, brilliant inventions while having fun. Allow your team to have fun creating success.

Planning is a very important ingredient for success. It may take the form of a group discussion in which the tasks to reach a goal are identified and assigned according to the abilities of those available. Even though "serious business" is being discussed, friendly humor helps to make the time enjoyable, to keep everyone's attention, to make people feel comfortable, and to build team spirit.

Wright

Is there more to the spiritual aspect of presence?

Dawson

Presence allows us to keep our focus on our daily lives while enjoying the magic of coincidences. Many people have stories of how unusual events or a gentle voice guiding them kept them safe. Have you ever been in a shop and noticed something by chance that you know a friend would appreciate? Listening to our hearts opens us up to intuitive guidance. We each have our own unique path in life and our own truth that changes as we grow. We can only feel fulfilled when we each choose what feels right to us based on what we know in our heart.

Our ultimate desire is for the success of every creature on Earth, Earth itself, and every other being that may exist elsewhere. There are many examples of this desire in trade agreements, choices to care for Earth and to protect the habitats of various species, and stories of humans and other animals saving humans. The more we see that this desire is built into the very fabric of existence, the easier it becomes to accept the things we wish to change.

The key to change is acceptance. Before we can make things different we must accept the way they are. Dr. Emoto's water crystal photographs show the affects of words on water. Physicists have shown that atoms—the building blocks of everything—obey our thoughts. Dr. Len, a psychologist, repeated, "I'm sorry" and "I love you" while studying the charts of insane patients in Hawaii. He found within himself how he had created each patient's illness, and all of the patients healed. Perhaps we dislike seeing pain and suffering because on some level we know that we are responsible for it and able to fix it.

Wright

This has been an interesting conversation. I appreciate the time you've taken, Gwen, to answer these questions.

We've been talking with Gwen Dawson. As a child, Gwen began looking for the truth in religions. Knowing many religions, she chose her beliefs based on what she felt in her heart. This was not only based on the information she had garnered from her surroundings. There was information to which her reality had to adhere that she knew from somewhere else. She has come to see life as an adventure with this source—an entity with many names including: divine intelligence, universal law, love, self, and God.

She has observed the sensitivity of children to the moods of others around them and seen that students' beliefs in their abilities have a greater influence on their success than their intelligence or understanding of a topic. She has been discussing how we can attain success by consciously placing our awareness.

ABOUT GWEN DAWSON

Gwen was born in Scotland, grew up in Jamaica, and then moved to Nevis. After teaching mathematics and physics for seven years in the Eastern Caribbean, she opened her own tutoring business on the beautiful island of Saba. She has observed the effect of her students' thoughts on their self-esteem and productivity. She asserts that success has more to do with confidence than abilities. She recommends a variety of techniques that she has found helpful, including meditation, energy therapies, and  breathing techniques and she guides others in expanding their awareness so that they notice and bring into their lives what will produce success.

Gwen Dawson
Bright Minds
Windwardside
Saba, Eastern Caribbean
599.522.2060
a.healthy.me@gmail.com
www.brightminds.00freehost.com

ROADMAP to SUCCESS 10

CAROL VAN BRUGGEN

David Wright (Wright)

Today we're talking with Carol Van Bruggen. As a familiar voice in the media, Carol's financial advice has appeared in special financial sections of numerous newspapers over the last twenty years. She has been featured on several radio stations as a business and finance reporter, talk show host, and guest. She has also appeared on numerous television specials and reports and has authored three books with the partners of her firm, Foord, Van Bruggen, Ebersole, and Pajak Financial Services. Carol is a certified financial planner and a public speaker who captivates and entertains her audience when she speaks. She addresses current financial trends and shares the secrets of creating an exciting vision for life using their undiscovered wealth.

Often called the "Wealth Vision Guide" she has assisted hundreds to discover what they really want out of life and how to make that vision a reality by following their own personal road map.

Carol, welcome to *Roadmap to Success.*

Carol, first, how did you get the nickname the Wealth Vision Guide?

Carol Van Bruggen (Van Bruggen)

I have been helping people create financial plans for over twenty-five years and I realized early on that before people could establish a plan to assure they had the resources they needed for lifetime "financial security" they needed to know exactly what that meant and how it would look when they got there.

Before running a bunch of numbers or even figuring out what our clients had to work with I would take them through what we call at my firm the "Discovery Process." In that process we determine what it is they want their life and the lives of those they care about to look like. Long after we presented their finished plan (or road map), and sometimes years later, the vision process and how we had developed it was what they remembered the most about the entire financial planning process. In fact, one planning client introduced me as his "Wealth Vision Guide" when I spoke to his Association, and the name stuck. I now include it as part of my introductions regularly. I also often sing a song when I speak that was written by a friend of mine called, "I've Got a Vision (for my life)."

Wright

How does one actually create a vision for his or her life?

Van Bruggen

There are two steps to creating a vision, an easy step and, for some, a more difficult step.

First one must make some time in a day to "daydream" with no distractions. Now, that's the hard part—finding the time to do some constructive dreaming. But without this step people will never get to their desired destination because they really don't know where they want to be.

Next, they must write down a vivid description of their vision as if it was five, ten, or fifteen years from now and they are living it. They must believe as they write that every word will come true. That's the easy part. People can have several visions and their visions can change over time. Like any journey, the trip takes us through different scenery and we may decide to stop at various vistas along the way, but what keeps us moving in the right direction is knowing that what we picture is up ahead.

Holding a clear vision of what you want, whether now or in the future, can be very powerful. Often desires that are intensely felt and written down actually take shape sooner than originally planned.

Wright

How can people know their vision will really make them happy if they were to attain it?

Van Bruggen

It is very important that when people create their vision they understand clearly why they want to see themselves living this picture they have in their mind. If they picture themselves as filthy rich with all the luxuries that life can offer, they might need to picture what they are doing to create that wealth. Are they alone or are there others around them as they play with the toys they can now afford to buy? Do they have the time to play when they are working so hard to make all that money? Why do they want riches? Do they see themselves as adored by their friends because they have money, or do they feel more secure now that bad things won't happen to them or their family because they have money? Perhaps what they really want is to have more friends and the ability to do more for their family. Maybe more money is not what will make them happy at all and they can do things right this moment to make their vision a reality.

Wright

What's the first step in making a vision a reality?

Van Bruggen

As with all journeys to a destination, people need to figure out exactly where they are now. We call that the "red dot" in life. Like the red dots on the map that indicate "you are here" as you enter a mall, if you know where you are it is certainly easier to figure out a plan to get to where you want to go. So in the most matter-of-fact way possible people need to make an assessment of where they are and what they have to work with.

Next they need to determine what is missing and put each item on their list in order or priority. For example: One may want to travel the world and work with wild animals. The person might currently run a construction company in a small town in the

Midwest. The first step toward making their vision a reality might be to look up volunteer opportunities available with an organization like Earth Watch or Biosphere. This would allow the person to travel someplace and work as a volunteer for an animal conservation project and learn more about how to do something like that full-time.

Wright

How do people map out their journey toward their vision?

Van Bruggen

After figuring out where your "red dot" is, you can then begin planning your journey. What will you need and where will you want to stop along the way?

Sometimes a journey is easier to plan if you have a guide or someone who has traveled along many of the same paths before. Having a coach can sometimes accelerate your traveling speed to your destination vision, and sometimes it just plain makes it easier. Think of coaches as vision tour guides. Coaches can save you money and time even though you may have to pay for their help. Just how badly you want your vision to become a realty will determine how committed you are to finding a coach.

Next, like all journeys, you map out a timeline and figure out where you want to be and when you want to be there. Visualize every step of the way what you will experience and what rations you will need at that point to go on further. If you come up blank occasionally, that's okay; some stops along the way will be a complete surprise but you'll know what to do next.

Wright

When you say "many people have undiscovered wealth" what exactly do you mean?

Van Bruggen

Over the years, as I've worked with clients in planning for financial independence, I have asked them to give me information on what they have managed to save and accumulate. But I also ask them about any opportunities or options they have that they have not yet taken advantage of such as contacts, discounts, and free money. Let me give you a couple of examples.

Often, someone who is working for a company might have the option of saving in a deferred compensation plan or 401(k). Within most pension plans participants can save up to $15,000 a year or more, but even more exciting, many companies match their savings with additional contributions up to a fixed percentage. Not taking advantage of this benefit is like throwing money away.

There are times we don't realize that who we know can be as important as what we know. If you have always wanted to raft down the Grand Canyon and you meet someone who is a guide in the summer or who has a friend who owns a rafting company, get in touch and tell him or her of your dream. That person may just be able to help you make the vision a reality sooner than you think.

Want to become a great public speaker? The chamber of commerce in your city may offer free or discounted "public speaking" courses if you are a member. If membership has its benefits, then take advantage of them.

Wright

What do you mean by the "fire of desire" and why do you think it is crucial to success in making a vision come true?

Van Bruggen

All truly successful people I know have told me that they couldn't help themselves from following their dream. My financial planning partner, Elfrena, always asks her clients a key question when they say to her they want something badly. She asks them, "Just how badly do you want it?" She says that if they don't have the "fire of desire" they will not stay the course when things get "iffy." So be sure you have the fire of desire or all the planning in the world won't put the fuel in your engine to keep going.

Wright

What do you mean when you say "keep focused on your vision but don't miss the lions in the grass"?

Van Bruggen

One vision I had for my life was a trip to Africa on a big game safari. I had watched Mutual of Omaha's *Wild Kingdom* since I was a little girl and pictured myself seeing the African "big five" up close and in real time. When I turned fifty my husband took me on my first trip to Botswana and we stayed in a wildlife refuge in the Okavanga Delta. I was excited to see all the animals I had seen on *Wild Kingdom*—the elephant, the hippo, the cape buffalo, giraffes. But one animal I really wanted to see was the cheetah. Every day we went out and looked for cheetahs. People would come back to camp at night and around the campfire they would tell us about their sightings of cheetahs that day. But, I never saw any.

One morning we were out on a game drive and as usual I was looking as hard as I could for a cheetah out on the open plain. The guides knew I really wanted to see one so they were looking through their binoculars to see if they could find one for me.

Sitting there in the jeep I could hear the birds—there are hundreds in Botswana—and I heard a guide whisper to me, "Missy Carol, don't miss the lions . . ." I didn't understand what he meant. I looked around and saw nothing. He nodded down to the grass next to the vehicle and there in the grass was a pride of over nineteen lions! I had been so focused on finding a cheetah I had almost missed the excitement of one of the most exciting times I remember in Africa.

This is so very much like life—we must have a vision and keep it in our mind, but we don't want to miss out on the excitement of what life brings our way as we travel in the direction of our dreams. And the journey may be what we remember the most. So I try to remind people to "keep focused, but don't miss the lions in the grass."

Wright

Okay, so how will we know when we are really living our vision for our life, and do some people get there and never even realize it?

Van Bruggen

My husband and I are big on visioning. We have even made what we call "treasure maps" out of photos from magazines pasted to cardboard and positioned somewhere in our home where we can see them. Over the last couple of years we laugh when we say, "Gee, wouldn't it be nice to have—" and then bring out our old maps to remind ourselves we now have everything we wanted when we made up our "treasure maps." We call this a "this isn't it" moment. This means that no matter what we might have, as human beings we are always looking to the horizon for something more. So now we do something else—we think of all the things we already have that we had dreamed of many years ago. It makes us realize how very grateful we are. It's a good exercise for everyone to do while they are creating their next vision.

Wright

What are the "4 C's" essential to making a vision for your life gratifying?

Van Bruggen

The four C's are: Clarity, Confidence, Contentment, and Contribution.

For any vision to be truly fulfilling people need to have *Clarity* for what they truly want. There is nothing worse than creating a vision and finding out it was not really all that it was cracked up to be after it became a reality.

Next, *Confidence* in our ability to control our own destiny makes for a much happier life—less stress, more time for enjoyment. Sometimes just knowing where we are along the path and what tools we have to get us where we want to go can give us the confidence we need.

Contentment is the part about not thinking we always need more. When a vision comes true let's take a little time to revel in our success. I always wanted to have a deck overlooking the river. It took many years, but now I have one and every time I go out to sit on my lounge chair I pretend I am on vacation.

Contribution means that life and visions are not very fulfilling unless we feel we are contributing to others in some way. One of the reasons we hear about so many of the rich and famous getting involved in good works these days is because having a lot of stuff and doing a million things can get old. Happiness comes from knowing we really have made a difference during the time we have been on this earth.

Wright

What do you mean when you say "wealth is more than money"?

Van Bruggen

Wealth can be many things. I think when people realize they can create a vision and can actually step into it today and make it happen, they might start with a financial vision. We tend to believe we can do just about anything if we just have enough money. But over the years, as I have counseled my clients on creating financial independence, I have found that true wealth really *is* way more than financial means. Wealth can be as simple as the talent or wisdom we are willing to share with others, family, and friends. The sooner we realize that, the better visions we will create for our lives and the more fun the journey along the way will be.

Wright

Tell us about the "Wealth and Beyond Program."

Van Bruggen

The Wealth and Beyond Program is a program my partners and I developed and have written about in our latest book with the working title of *Wealth and Beyond, Discovering the Treasures of Wealth.* The program evokes in people the desire to create an exciting vision for their lives using the wealth they have come to realize they possess. We are happy that after over twenty five years of working with our clients to help them create financial wealth, we can now help them discover what they can do to make that wealth go on to provide a foundation for the betterment of others.

ABOUT CAROL VAN BRUGGEN

Carol Van Bruggen, CFP, is a Certified Financial Planner and a partner in the firm of Foord, Van Bruggen, Ebersole, and Pajak Financial Services. Carol has been a consultant to business and professional clients for over twenty-five years, earning the nickname the "Wealth Vision Guide."

She has co-authored three books with her financial partners, the latest, *Wealth and Beyond, Discovering the Treasures of Wealth,* shares experiences of their clients as they worked to become comfortable with wealth and create a vision for their life.

Carol has been a regular on several local radio and television stations with financial commentary and is a professional speaker.

She has served on numerous non-profit and professional boards of directors over the years and is an advocate of the arts, particularly in education. In addition to her financial advisory firm, Carol owns a technology firm called ERC Systems, which installs cost effective online directories of local artists, performers, and film professionals for arts agencies nationwide.

She travels regularly to Africa and takes groups there to contribute time and money to the needs of African people. Carol's husband, Steve Kuhn, owns and runs a small Marina in Sacramento and is her number one fan when she practices her love of singing.

Carol Van Bruggen, CFP
Foord, Van Bruggen, Ebersole, and Pajak Financial Services
2255 Watt Ave., Ste. 300
Sacramento, CA 95825
916.487.8700, Ext. 3
cvb@fvbe.info
www.WealthAndBeyondProgrm.com

ROADMAP *to* SUCCESS 11

An interview with ...

BILL JENSEN

David Wright (Wright)

Today we're talking with Bill Jensen, more famously know as Mr. Simplicity. Bill is today's foremost expert on work complexity and cutting through clutter to what really matters. He's CEO of the Jensen Group and has authored four books, including 2000's bestseller, *Simplicity*. For over a decade, you've been researching   the impact on the generational shift we're now beginning to see in our workplace. Why is this shift so important?

Bill Jensen (Jensen)

A tipping point is fast approaching: Globally, GenY will soon reach critical mass as workers just as Boomers leave in mass numbers. There will be a changing of the guard. In the United States it's more than 70 million Boomers retiring or refocusing their careers as more than 70 million GenYers enter the workforce. While the basics of leadership will never change, GenY will most certainly redraw today's road map. We need to talk about this as both a warning that you must change if you want GenY to follow where you lead, and as a set of milestones you can use for planning tomorrow's road map.

GenY is the first generation in human history—no, that's not an exaggeration—who have been raised on, and trained to expect, the total democratization of information. While Boomers are still running companies where everything must flow from the top down, GenY will expect Google-like transparency and total access to anything and everything. They will expect instant information and decision-making that is useful and meaningful *to them* and socially blessed *by them.*

Ultimately this transition is about a major shift from being mostly corporate-centered in what we design to getting work done to being far more user-centered.

Right now, most corporate systems are still designed to save the *company* time, to invest the *company's* assets wisely, to reduce the *company's* costs, etc. As GenY reaches critical mass, if companies want those things, they're *also* going to have to respect each *individual's* time and invest all the *individual's* assets wisely—in a knowledge- and service-work economy, they *are* the means of production—continually focusing on making it easier for each individual to get their work done. This is easier from the *individual's* perspective, not necessarily from the leader's.

Wright

So, clearly, to meet the needs of this new generation, we must change how we build companies and how we create work tools, but is this truly a shift in how leaders must lead?

Jensen

Absolutely! This is the age-old management versus leadership debate. Building tomorrow's infrastructures is definitely a management task. But what sets leaders apart from managers is their ability to see and engage others in a future that is distinct from the past. Leaders create a vision of that future. They initiate and nurture conversations and questions that change how we look at that future, and they drive changes in how we will experience that future. That is what is immediately required of today's leaders—*to initiate and nurture completely new conversations* about the changes that GenY and their democratizing technologies are forcing upon our organizations.

Jensen Group research has uncovered three *huge* strategic issues that are likely to determine the winners and losers in the global war for talent for the next decade or two!

Wright

And those big strategic issues are?

Jensen

1. The rights and needs of the individual versus the rights and needs of the organization
2. The rights and needs and ownership of communities
3. How we address major gaps in fundamental skills

Let me unpack each of those.

First, the rights and needs of the individual versus the rights and needs of the organization: this is the über issue—everything else cascades from this one. For thousands of years, since the first leaders led the first organizations, it's been mostly a one-way deal—the way we did things was the leader's way. Then, for the last hundred years or so, modern management practices directed many of our daily work activities. Process and procedure ruled the day. Over the past few decades, we've since seen great progress in the areas of teamwork, empowerment, and individual autonomy.

But this is not enough for GenY. Many of the tools we use to measure, manage, motivate, train, and develop today's workforce seem hopelessly outdated and wasteful to them. That's because these tools are still *corporate-centered*. They are designed to first meet the organization's needs, with the expectation that each individual's work needs—how they learn, how they make decisions, how they make sense of everything coming at them, how they are managed—all flow from what others have decided is the best approach.

GenY sees this as a leadership failure.

Wright

Doing what's best for the organization as a whole—where's the leadership failure in that?

Jensen

As you framed it, it's no failure at all. But GenY doesn't see this as an either/or debate—*either* we build what's best for corporate-wide practices *or* we build what's best for each individual.

This generation knows that it is possible to design learning and working tools that are completely tailored for them *and* serve the greater community. They know this because they've been living this approach their whole life as students, as friends and family, and as consumers.

Take any function or practice inside your company—managing projects, building a team, daily communication, building a community, building consensus and commitment, managing investments, checking inventory, logging expenses—by the time they are twenty-five years old, the average GenYer has already experienced hundreds of ways to tailor these experiences to make the most of their skills, their tools, and their way of working, greatly enhancing their personal effectiveness, productivity, and efficiency. This was never possible on a large scale before their generation—the full democratization of information and user-centered tools has been within reach of the average consumer only for the past two decades.

Yet how many of today's leaders truly *get* this change? Heck, millions of iPhone owners can't even get their IT departments to acknowledge that this tool exists, and that's the babiest of baby steps that GenY is seeking! If you're a leader and you want to win the war for GenY talent, you've got to be focused on the shift toward individual ways of working. You've got to be driving completely new conversations about this future.

Wright

So, even though the driver of the upcoming changes is technology, your research says that it's really about the changing role of leadership?

Jensen

Yes. It's really about who will set the agenda for more equal control of a working relationship. Must it be forced from the bottom up, through high turnover rates or will leaders drive the need for change first?

If the trends that we're seeing continue (and there's no reason to assume they won't) during the coming decade—2010 to 2020—we will see a new shift in the relationship between worker and company. Gartner Research concurs. Their 2006 study, *Extreme Individualization*, pointed to the same conclusions as my firm's study, *Search for a Simpler Way*: These studies reveal that the working contract will move beyond the usual—compensation, role, duties, benefits—to also include how work actually gets done. GenY will look for a lot more My Work My Way. And why not? Ultimately, in a knowledge and service economy, having work tools and information flows that make every individual more productive, efficient, and effective benefit the company even more.

Big issues in this generation's parents' day were diversity, teamwork, and empowerment. But the Boomers, on the whole, were willing to wait for leaders to drive these issues. GenY won't be so patient. They'll vote with their feet. In many companies, this shift will unfortunately occur only when they need to triage high turnover rates, not before.

Wright

You've gone into depth about what your research has shown to be the number one issue. Will you provide an overview of the other two big issues?

Jensen

Each springs out of the efforts of focusing on the needs of the individual.

The second major issue is the rights and needs and ownership of communities. Technology is helping every worker bring a valuable asset into the relationship with your company—his or her social network. Often, these networks and communities are how things really get done. In the past, the company was the owner of community in how it organized teams and departments and divisions. Now, those formal connections are becoming less important than the rich networks and social connections built and maintained by each employee. Today's leaders must acknowledge who owns those communities, and their infrastructures and processes need to reflect the workers' rights and ownership.

The other major issue is how we address major gaps in fundamental skills. According to the Pew Charitable Trust, in the United States, about half of GenY will be entering the workforce without the skills they need to do the complex analysis and reasoning their jobs require or to do the simple, clear communication that others will require of them.

GenY will be experiencing the most information-rich work environment ever, and sadly, many will be under-prepared by the educational system. They will need lots of support in the fundamentals that leaders feel, rightfully so, should have been covered by educational institutions. But there simply aren't enough workers in this generation prepared to quickly *and* deeply analyze, then translate, think through, and clearly communicate all the daily complexities they will encounter.

Wright

Taking all three of those big issues together, are there any examples of how this shift has already begun to spread?

Jensen

UPS was among the earliest large employers to feel the impact of this shift. In 2003, when the oldest GenYers started applying for jobs, UPS noticed a serious decline in key performance indicators. Teaching their "340 methods"—a detailed manual of rules and routines—through lectures, just didn't work anymore. Previous new-hires took about thirty days to become proficient drivers. GenYers were taking ninety to one hundred and eighty days. Since this generation would make up over 60 percent of the company's part-time loader workforce, if they didn't act quickly, this shift could have drastically impacted their bottom line.

The company invested over three years overhauling its training to meet the needs of GenYers. They didn't lower their standards; instead, they changed how they personalized and delivered the training. Teams of UPS executives, professors, and design students at Virginia Tech, a team from MIT, forecasters from the Institute of the Future, and animators all collaborated to meet the needs of this new workforce. And because UPS received $1.8 million from the U.S. Department of Labor, much of the data, including research related to safety and generational differences will be made public.

GenYers are great disbelievers: "Prove it to me. Prove me or you right; prove me or you wrong." So UPS designed video and data-driven proof of rights and wrongs—real-time personalized feedback, whereas in the past, trainees were expected to accept the wisdom of the trainer at face value, that is no longer the case.

Another example of this shift is at India's HCL Technologies. The usual approach to 360-degree feedback for executives is that it's all behind closed doors—no executive wants all their warts and imperfections openly shared! Not at HCL. Vineet Nayar, CEO, and his top twenty managers' 360-degree feedback scores are all published on the company's intranet for all to see. This is the kind of transparency that GenY will expect to see.

146

A great example of a missed opportunity, so far, is at P&G. CEO A. J. Lafely, along with management guru Ram Charam, talk about the power of the customer in their book, *Game Changer.* Lafely's organization is continually given high praise for leadership development, and deserves credit for pushing the boundaries of innovation by getting much closer to its customers. Yet, while the company proudly touts stories of studying the daily habits of Mexican housewives to improve how they make and sell soap, they haven't shown the same amount of due diligence in listening to their own workforce.

GenY workers want to be heard. They will expect leaders to spend as much time listening to them as they do to the firm's most profitable and most important customers. Connie Moore, from Forrester Research, says that paying attention to their needs for personalized work tools is critical as they "create a 360-degree view of business processes, as unstructured and structured information."

My Work My Way doesn't disrupt standardized, centralized processes. It's more about each individual's need for personalized sense making, meaning making, and decision-making. That need will only grow as business environments become more and more complex.

Wright

So if leaders want to get ahead of this shift, what can they do to get started?

Jensen

First, know that now is the time! While this shift has already begun, it's a couple years before GenY hits critical mass. So any leader starting right now should be well positioned for the tipping point of the major changes.

While it's still too early to point to the absolute best practices, there are some trends that are likely to drive this shift. What's required *right now* is to sponsor completely new conversations about how these trends will be incorporated into your business. Encouraging new questions and new debate is the wise leader's first step.

Big Idea 1: User-centered Design Moves from Marketplace to Workplace

Companies have figured out that making it easier for the customer to buy things helps them sell more and win in the marketplace. Those with the highest customer satisfaction and brand loyalty invest heavily in designing backward from the needs of those customers. And yet, because those same companies believe they have the right to use employees' time and attention as they see fit, the investment in user-centered research and development *inside* the company is currently next to nil. If you want to keep GenY, this *must* change. Making it as easy for employees to get things done will become as important as making it easier for customers to buy products. The art and science of user-centered design inside companies is likely to explode over the next decade.

Big Idea 2: Meaning-Making and Sense-Making Shifts from the Company to the Individual

In most companies, the C-suite still wants to be the main sense-maker—marketplace trends, customer trends, cost trends, productivity trends all get analyzed by senior executives and then coordinated and cascaded through the strategic plan and the business plan.

Business tools like strategic planning will not go away, but the antiquated model of driving sense making, decision-making, and evaluation solely through a hierarchical structure simply won't work for GenY. The big solution will be in giving GenY the tools and training they need so see they can see a lot more for themselves—the patterns and trends in the marketplace, in the company, in their customers, and in themselves. End result: they will be able to compare team goals, corporate goals, values, and more *by themselves, for themselves* so they can auto-adjust more, better, faster.

While exciting advances in analytics have already occurred with mind maps, social network maps, behavior mapping, and more, the real changes won't technological. The big shift will be in leadership attitudes toward transparency. Even though individuals *absolutely have to have* personalized tools to quickly make sense of the complex environs they work in, companies are still reticent to make corporate data so transparent and so easy to use by the average worker-bee—too much possibility for destructive use of the info.

That will be the design challenge—finding ways to give people access to what they need, how they need it, *without* compromising company security issues.

Big Idea 3: Training and Development Finally Gets User-centered

GenY will value their own training and development as highly as any other factor for staying at or leaving a company. If they're not being developed properly, learning enough, or growing enough, they'll simply leave.

Satisfying GenY won't mean that T&D will go all video-gamey. It will mean an extremely sophisticated and personalized approach to how each individual learns. As mentioned earlier, a great example of this shift is the millions of dollars of R&D and personalization that UPS recently launched in how it trains its drivers.

Another unfortunate but critical dimension of the new approach to training and development for GenY will be large corporate investments in the fundamentals:

- Critical thinking skills
- Communication skills
- Synthesizing and Organizing skills

Corporations will have to jump in where educational systems have not.

Big Idea 4: Organizational Chart Marries Social Networks

Most companies still rely on their organization chart to point to where power, control, authority, and accountability lie. Not only is technology creating a revolution in how people connect and collaborate with each other, but behind the latest technologies is the quickly maturing art and science of mapping and understanding and leveraging the connections within social networks. GenYers, like their predecessors, will want to know who's in charge, who's accountable, who the go-to people are, who's a potential resource and teammate, but they'll approach it differently than their predecessors. They'll want and need an integrated marriage between social network maps and today's organizational charts.

Big Idea 5: The Science and Discipline of Attention Moves from Marketplace to Workplace

What's the reason most companies are still serving "Death by PowerPoint"? It's not because of the technology! It's because of the *assumption* that the company has the right to use an employee's attention as it sees fit. ("You need to get this information in this way. Now, watch my presentation.") And yet, these same companies recognize that consumers will pay attention only to whatever they want and only how they want.

Consequently, the art and science of capturing and keeping the attention of the consumer is growing more sophisticated and competitive every day, while employees' attention is mostly taken for granted.

GenY will forever blow up this paradox. "Earn my attention all the time or else—"

An example of where this will head is YouTube's Insight. Video creators can now see for free very detailed statistics about everyone who viewed their video. On launching the service, YouTube said one way Insight was used was by musical bands to discover large fan bases in specific locations where they'd never visited. The bands then changed their tours accordingly.

GenY managers will want data on how to capture and keep the attention of everyone. Attention inside the company will become as hugely valued and closely monitored as it is outside the company.

Wright

Do you have any final guiding principles that will help leaders succeed as they take on this shift?

Jensen

First, listen. Really listen.

Your employees want to do their best for you. And they need your best in return. Change the dialogue and then really listen. You'll find that they're not bitching and moaning. The help they need and the changes they'll demand are all about increasing their own productivity, efficiency, and effectiveness. If you're willing to listen, the next generation of workers will guide you through all you need to know. Then, simplify, simplify, simplify; but differently than you do right now. Most simplicity inside most companies is still corporate-centered. Listen to how your workforce defines simplicity, and then design backward from there, making everything easier to use, easier to succeed.

Finally, have fun! Think about any three products in your life that you'd define as simple, easy to use, helpful, and that were designed backward from your needs. I'll guarantee a big smile will come to your face. That's the way to approach this shift— make things easier to use and succeeding becomes more fun!

ABOUT BILL JENSEN

Harvard Business Review, CNBC and *Fast Company* have called Bill Jensen today's foremost expert on work complexity and cutting through clutter to what really matters.

He has spent the past two decades studying how work gets done. (Much of what he's found horrifies him.) In his ongoing study, *The Search for a Simpler Way*, he has interviewed and surveyed over 500,000 workers around the globe. For the past decade, he has intensely focused on how GenY will forever change how we work.

He is an internationally-acclaimed author and speaker who is known for provocative ideas, extremely useful content, and his passion for making it easier for everyone to work smarter, not harder.

His first book, *Simplicity*, was the Number 5 Leadership/Management book on Amazon in 2000. His next best-seller is *Simplicity Survival Handbook: 32 Ways to Do Less and Accomplish More.*

His latest book, *What is Your Life's Work?*, captures the intimate exchanges between mothers and daughters, fathers and sons, and caring teammates, all talking about what matters at work, and in life.

Bill holds degrees in Communication Design and Organizational Development. He is CEO of The Jensen Group, whose mission is: To make it easier to get stuff done.

Among the Jensen Group's clients are Bank of America, Merck, Pfizer, GE, Genentech, NASA, The World Bank, Walt Disney World, American Express, British Petroleum, the US Navy SEALS, the government of Ontario, Singapore Institute of Management, Guangzhou China Development District, and the Swedish Post Office.

Bill's personal life fantasy is to bicycle around the globe via breweries.

Bill Jensen
The Jensen Group
1 Franklin Place
Morristown, NJ 07960
(973) 539-5070
bill@simplerwork.com

ROADMAP *to* SUCCESS

12

An interview with ...

CRAIG HOHNBERGER

David Wright (Wright)

Today we're talking with Craig Hohnberger. Craig is a dynamic and passionate leader, speaker, and entrepreneur with a passion for growing and developing businesses, the people who own them, and the teams that run them. After a successful corporate career he felt the call to go into business for himself and in 2001 purchased the Indiana and Central & Southern Ohio master franchise rights to develop ActionCOACH, a small little-known Australian company looking to expand in the United States. ActionCOACH has since grown into the world's number one business coaching firm, and Craig has proven to be one of the more successful master franchise owners in all of ActionCOACH. His territory of business coaches has produced numerous awards, including Global Franchise Owner of the Year, Best Client Results in North America, Rookie of the Year, Team Player of the Year, and several prestigious Action Man awards. In addition, his territory has been recognized as the United States Territory of the Year and was recently named a finalist for Global Territory of the Year. Craig, along with his wife and business partner, Annette, have also been awarded the Global Action Couple of the Year. In addition, he won New Business of the Year in his local Chamber of Commerce; he has been a member of the board of directors for the

Ohio Small Business Council, and was named to the Central Ohio 40 Under 40 Business Professionals for 2004.

Craig, welcome to *Roadmap to Success*!

Craig Hohnberger (Hohnberger)

Thanks, David; it's a pleasure to be here!

Wright

What did you do prior to ActionCOACH?

Hohnberger

I was a supply chain executive in a corporate environment, primarily with a number of large Fortune 200 companies including Pillsbury, GE, and Newell-Rubbermaid, along with a large, privately-held company. I originally started on the engineering side but most of my corporate life was in operations and supply chain management, with a number of years involved in corporate acquisitions. We'd buy companies, and I'd go in and help turn them around and integrate them into our main business. I had a lot of fun and a great corporate career.

Wright

Why did you decide to leave your corporate life?

Hohnberger

Well, David, looking back, several things led to it. As a kid, my mom always encouraged me to own a business, so the desire had always been in the back of my mind and in my heart. Then I remember one year where we only made eighteen and a half cents per share in earnings and the analysts had predicted nineteen cents. We made a whole lot of money that year, but because we didn't quite make as much as some twenty-six-year-old kids on Wall Street thought we were going to make, we laid off a lot of people, negatively affecting all of those lives and their families. And finally, an integration project I was on required me to stay two weeks at a time. It was a full day flight each way, so instead of burning two days in the air each week, I'd stay through the weekend and work a second week before coming home for a week; then I'd go back on the road again.

Well, on the second day of one of those trips. My wife, Annette, called me and said, "Guess what, Lauren (my daughter) took her first steps!" I'll tell you, David, I just started crying, I didn't know what else to do. This was a big moment of her life and mine that I'll never experience—that I'll never get back. So I started to question *why* I was doing what I was doing.

Eleven days later, on the flight home, I had the blessing of sitting next to an older couple who were in their mid-seventies and returning from vacation. Rose was sitting next to me and her husband, Ralph, was sitting next to her. It was a long flight so we started chatting and I got to know them and was showing them pictures of my young family. When I was explaining that I couldn't wait to get home to see my daughter because she had just learned how to walk while I was on this trip, I could sense that Rose wanted to give me some life advice but didn't want to intrude; she was biting her tongue a little bit. So I finally looked at her and said, "Rose, what advice would you give a young guy like me who's really starting to hit his stride career-wise and at the same time building his family?"

Rose asked, "Craig, do you really want to know?"

"Yeah, I do," I replied.

Ralph leaned over and said, "You asked for it!" He knew his wife pretty well.

For the next six hours, it was a fire-hose of life stories and advice. As we prepared to land in Chicago, Rose asked me, "Craig, we'll never see each other again, so would it be okay if I share the essence of what we have been talking about?"

I said, "Yes, Rose, I would love that."

She continued with some of the best advice I have ever been given; it literally changed my life, although I didn't fully appreciate it at the time. Rose said, "To sum it all up, there are three things you need to do, Craig, if you want to get to our age and have no regrets."

And, David, both Rose and Ralph said that the *worst* part about being their age is the regrets they have. They can live with the aches and pains and the failures and losses they experienced in life, but the regrets are the toughest.

I said, "Okay, what are those three things?"

Rose started, "First, you need to take the time to invest in and truly love other people and develop relationships. You've got to start with your kids and your family, as they are closest to you. And you can't do it from Puerto Rico." She told me something that I've never forgotten: "Craig, always remember, your kids don't spell love 'l-o-v-e,' they spell it 't-i-m-e' "! She also said that the common practice of parents justifying time away from their family by talking about quality time being more important than quantity of time is quite frankly B.S. The bottom line is that all your kids want is you in their life and for you to be there for them!

She said, "Number two: pursue your dreams, whatever your dreams happen to be. And if you don't mind me being frank with you, it looks like you're pursuing your company's dreams right now; so my advice is to get clarity on your own dreams and go after them."

And thirdly, she said, "Take more risks. Don't let fear stop you. Don't get to be our age and wonder *'what if?'* Ralph and I will certainly not go to our graves wishing we'd played life safer. On the contrary, we wish we had gone after it."

She concluded by telling me, "If you do those three things, you'll get to our age and have no regrets. Life will have been worth living."

Basically, she planted the seeds and put enough water on them so they'd keep growing, and that's what started me on my journey to decide what I really wanted to be "when I grew up."

Wright

So did you leave your corporate life at that time?

Hohnberger

No, but I immediately stopped all the travel. During the next several years I bounced around a lot. Looking back, I think I was searching for the "holy grail" of a corporate career. I wanted the upward mobility, the income, and the balance with my personal life. I wanted to work with and for people I truly respected—for a company I believed in—doing something I was passionate about, and I wanted a career that fully leveraged my gifts, passions, and abilities. I wanted it all. It just seemed that at every stop during my corporate life, to be successful and fit in, I had to compromise a big part of my personal goals and who I was. I couldn't seem to find somewhere I could put it *all* together.

Finally I decided, "I've got to find something that gives me *everything* I want," and to do so I realized that I would have to be the guy in charge, so I started looking into a lot of businesses.

Wright

What kinds of businesses did you look at?

Hohnberger

I looked at a lot—everything from starting my own consulting business doing what I did in my corporate life, to a landscaping company, a concrete manufacturing company, transmission shops, restaurants, franchises and non-franchises—you name it! I didn't really care what the actual product or service was. In my corporate life, I worked for companies that made everything from injection molded products to food to glassware to large medical equipment. It really didn't matter to me, I just really enjoyed business, leadership, and developing businesses and teams. So, I looked at almost anything, and my criteria list at the time was pretty short. I was thinking, "so long as I'm the boss and can bring the cultural values and integrity that I want and can make enough income to support my lifestyle goals," then the business should go on the list. And as you know, David, there are *thousands* of ways to make money in the world, so the list kept getting longer.

Wright

It sounds like a lot; how did you keep track of it all?

Hohnberger

Trying to make it as objective as possible, I actually set up a T-account with pros and cons on each one and a scoring matrix for the key things. For instance, income was worth ten out of ten and working hours were worth eight out of ten and so on. So I actually had a score for each business I looked at. I thought it was a good process, but I was getting more confused because so many things started blurring together.

Then I called an old boss of mine, Mike, for some advice. He was a really great mentor through the years and had given me some great career advice that I sometimes took and sometimes didn't, but Mike always seemed to understand me really well. So I asked him what businesses he felt I'd be best at and I shared some of those I was most interested in at the time.

Mike asked, "Craig, how many different things are you looking at?" I told him there were probably thirty or so on the list somewhere, and probably six or eight that I was looking at in depth at any given time.

"You know, Craig," he said, "this T-account thing is really stupid."

"That's why I called you, Mike; give me some advice."

Mike continued, "You're wasting valuable time and energy and your own personal resources comparing your twentieth best opportunity with your tenth best opportunity with your best opportunity. What you really need to do is first sit down and figure out who the heck you are and what you really want out of life. And then pick the opportunity that comes closest. Research that one inside out and if it can get you there, go for it. Going into business will be a big commitment no matter what, but I know you well enough to know that you have the work ethic and raw ability to be successful if it *can* get you there. If it can't, then move on to number two."

Mike's straightforward advice about understanding my own goals actually tied right into what Rose had told me several years earlier.

Wright

What led you to decide ActionCOACH was the right fit?

Hohnberger

Taking Mike's advice, I sat down one weekend with a legal pad and I asked myself, "Who am I and what do I want? If I'm going to go into business for myself, what does the *perfect* business look like for me?" And I just started writing. Of course, income and the ability to create wealth were on the list among several other key things. Then I started asking myself even deeper, more important questions like, "What kind of people do I want to be around—customers, employees, and colleagues? What kind of relationships do I want to have with those people? What kind of working hours do I want? What type of product or service? What industry? What kind of impact do I want to have in the world? What legacy do I want to leave for my kids? What do I want to learn, if anything? What will a perfect day look like to me?" And these questions started to bring me a lot more clarity.

As I answered these questions, I started building my perfect business. I realized that I definitely wanted business-to-business. Other people might prefer business-to-consumer, but I wanted normal business hours and wanted to deal with business people versus the general public. I also wanted to work with the decision-makers. I didn't want to talk to a purchasing person who has to run it up a chain to get somebody else to make the decision, I wanted to actually deal with the decision-maker—the

CEO, president, or the owner of the company. I wanted a smaller group of high-performance employees, but I wanted deeper personal relationships with those employees versus having lots of employees with transactional type relationships. I wanted passionate employees who would challenge me and make me better just because they are on my team.

In my last corporate job there were several hundred employees who reported in through my function and unfortunately I didn't get the chance to have deep relationships with many of them. I also realized that if it really was the *perfect* business for me, I'd also have those same kinds of relationships with my customers and colleagues as I did with my employees—less transactional in nature and deeper, longer lasting, and more personal.

Some of the other key things I wanted were lots of variety and flexibility, as I don't like routine. I wanted something more people-oriented and not very administratively burdensome or technical in nature. I wanted to be able to travel, but on my schedule and to places I like to travel, versus my corporate days where I hated traveling because someone said I had to and the locations were not necessarily where I wanted to go.

I wanted a business with high profit margins and lower volume, versus a commodity that was high volume with lower profit margin. I wanted a growing industry—one where I was part of the best of the best, and I wanted a business that inherently had great people around me who would challenge me to really step up my game and be the best I could be. I wanted something that forced me to grow and develop myself—to build skills and provide additional opportunities for the future. And ultimately, I wanted something that would allow me to leave a legacy of truly helping people, making a difference in their lives, and making the world a better place.

After doing this exercise and really gaining clarity for myself, it was quite obvious that ActionCOACH was the best fit for me. I really wish I'd done this a lot earlier in the process, as it would have saved me a lot of time and energy.

Wright

How did you find ActionCOACH in the first place?

Hohnberger

As I was looking for the right business, I came across an ad that said "Wanted, People with Passion. People with Heart: Use your business and leadership skills and experiences coupled with our proven systems and methodologies to help other business owners achieve their goals." And I thought, "Wow, that sounds intriguing." So as I went through the due diligence process thoroughly, I found that it was the perfect fit for me. I thank God that it was an opportunity I found as I went through my soul-searching process.

Wright

Most people who are looking for a job are looking for the hours and money, they never seem to think about the fact that you become like the people you are around. So I'm glad you really thought through that. I'm really excited about your finding ActionCOACH, but what exactly does ActionCOACH do?

Hohnberger

We are a global business coaching franchise company with now over one thousand offices in twenty-six countries. We're coaching over fifteen thousand businesses every week. I own a Master Franchise with ActionCOACH.

What we do is work with the owners and key executives of businesses to help them achieve their goals in life by setting up their businesses to get them there. A key business philosophy we hold is that the business ought to give the owners of the business whatever their life goals and ambitions happen to be. At the end of the day the business is nothing more than a vehicle to help them achieve their life goals. So it starts with the question, "What do you really want out of life, Mr. or Mrs. Client, and how do we set up and structure your business to get you there?" And that all boils down to gaining clarity on their goals and dreams, making the money to fund those goals and dreams, and freeing up their hours so they can spend their time doing those things they really want to do, whether it's travel or golf, hanging out with the kids or grandkids, getting involved in charities and volunteer organizations, or building more businesses. Everyone's goal is different.

We have a powerful model with 428 methodologies and strategies, delivered in a coaching relationship, to teach them how to systematically grow their business to make more money, how to put the right systems in place to leverage their businesses further, and how to hire, develop, and retain the right employees to free up their time as owners. Ultimately, if they choose, owners can even build their business to where it can work without having to be there to run it. This significantly increases their choices as well as the value of their business. But it all starts with their goals.

Wright

So, your clients, then, would be people who own or manage their own business, right?

Hohnberger

Correct. Our bread-and-butter clients are people who currently own and operate their own business and have been in business for several years or even for several generations. We also work with the executives of larger corporations as well some start-ups. It really depends on the individual franchise owner on what they get most excited about and who they most want to work with and help.

We have group mentoring programs, one-to-one mentoring programs, and even some training products like books, DVDs, and business games. We have something at every price point and for every business. But I would definitely say our signature programs are our one-to-one mentoring programs where our coaches work with the business owners in an ongoing relationship that may span years, in part coaching and teaching them what to do and how to do it, and in part holding them accountable to get it done.

Wright

What is your role as a Master Franchise Owner?

Hohnberger

As the Master Franchise Owner I have the Territory Development Franchise for the Ohio and Indiana region. My team's job is to recruit, qualify, and select the right people who will make great ActionCOACH franchise owners and then help coach and support them in successfully building their businesses.

Wright

So you actually recruit people who do the business coaching?

Hohnberger

Correct. I recruit and qualify the people who will own a business coaching franchise within our region. They get all of our global systems and training and support and my office also provides localized support for them.

Wright

When you discussed it a little bit before, why didn't you try to do it on your own outside of a franchise?

Hohnberger

A great question, David. That was probably one of my biggest questions when I started looking at the franchise, especially given my need to be in a more unstructured environment. Thankfully, the ActionCOACH franchise is not all that structured. It provides a lot of creative and innovative expression, and you can basically create what you want out of it.

The other thing that attracted me initially was the sheer success rates of franchising in general. Statistics indicate over 90 percent of businesses that start up outside of a franchise will fail in a few short years, versus over a 75 percent success rate in franchises.

I also realized a couple of key things. Number one was that I didn't have access to all of the tools and knowledge they'd been developing for many years prior. All I had was what was in my head. If I truly believed in helping people as much as possible, wouldn't I want to provide them with the best of the best tools and resources available?

Number two, the training, the support, the culture, etc., were very strong. I know myself well enough to know, especially coming out of a Fortune 200 type of background, that I function well and really enjoy being in a collaborative team—a collegiate type of environment. I didn't want to be the only person committed to my own success, I wanted to have a whole team around me with that success in mind, and ActionCOACH provides that. The growth of the brand over time would also play an important part because the world loves and trusts brands.

When I started, there were maybe forty offices around the world; now there are over one thousand. We literally have everything ActionCOACH provided originally, plus all the experience and innovation of all those years of our franchise owners. It's proven to be a really good decision; there's no way I could have duplicated what the franchise provided on day one, much less all the growth and innovation that I have access to now, seven years later.

In general, knowing what I know now, I would encourage anyone interested in a business to go the franchise route for their first couple of businesses for sure. Business ownership is not easy, but at least in a franchise environment, you don't have to do *everything* yourself. There is a big reason franchises are so much more successful than independent businesses. Just do your due diligence and be sure you pick the right one.

Wright

Would you tell our readers in what way this has so dramatically affected your life?

Hohnberger

This has influenced my life profoundly! It has certainly made me a much better businessperson than I ever could have been otherwise. I love business. I had a great business career prior, but I'd venture to guess that probably 80 to 85 percent of what I know about business today, I've learned since I've come to ActionCOACH. But even more importantly, it's made me a better father and a better husband—a better leader in my own family—because so much of what I've learned at ActionCOACH applies to being successful in all facets of life.

It's grown my vision in ways far beyond what I had ever imagined before. I would have been content making a certain level of income and doing something reasonably fun. Now my vision is much larger. Charities and philanthropy and things of that nature are a big part of what I'm doing and what I'm using this business to create. I'll give a little plug for us here: anybody who goes into a business or who is in any kind of business ought to consider hiring ActionCOACH, no matter what business you're in. The return on investment, both financial and otherwise, will be well worth it. It really is life changing. I've actually had clients thank me for helping them become better fathers, and others thank me for recruiting and inviting their coaches to join our team because those coaches have changed their life while helping them massively improve their business. It truly is amazing, the impact we have. I am actually interviewing a couple of clients who have been so impressed with the program that they want to join the team by buying a franchise and helping others do the same. That's powerful.

Wright

So what advice would you give someone else looking to go into business for themselves?

Hohnberger

The first bit of advice I'd say is get to know yourself. Do the very exercise I mentioned earlier. Ask yourself the really big questions: "What does that perfect business look like for me? What kind people do I want to be around? Do I want lots of employees or just a few? Higher performance employees or people who are just punching a clock? What kind of relationships do I want to have with those people? Do I prefer transactional relationships or do I want more personal, deeper relationships with people? What kind of product or service would I actually be passionate about? Do I prefer working with things or with ideas? What kinds of working hours? Where do I want to be in ten or fifteen years, and what's the right steppingstone that will help me get there? Do I want to be in a commodity-driven business that's very price-point sensitive or do I want to be in a service type of business that typically has more profit margin? Do I want to be with decision-makers or do I get intimidated by decision-makers and prefer selling to the general public or to a purchasing clerk? Do I want to grow and develop skills for the future or do I just want to earn an income? Am I willing to work hard for my success? Am I willing to hire people or outsource some things to offset the personal challenges and weaknesses I have?" It's really about getting to know yourself a lot better. Just start with a legal pad and start asking yourself the big questions.

Also, take the time to understand your fears. Fear is nothing more than a fear of the unknown. Identify what your fears are and educate yourself. Read books on business, success, and fear management as well as specific skills you may need to develop like sales or finance. (I let fear stop me for too long.) Then look at some businesses that appear to come close to your perfect model. If you've never owned a business or have only owned a few, focus on franchises to really hedge your success and mitigate risk. Research them and go for it when you find the one what comes closest. There are a lot of great franchise brokers who can help identify a great business that fits your goals and style.

Build a realistic financial model to get through the initial start-up curve. And be sure to budget the time and expense to travel and observe those who have achieved the goals you've set for yourself. Learn from them—learn from both their successes and mistakes—to get a head start. And there is no better learning than getting out there with those who are already successful.

And (another plug for us), no matter what business you choose, you'd be crazy not hire an ActionCOACH and get involved with our programs. Our programs really are powerful and will, at a minimum, set you up with what you need to do to be successful. At the very least, find a mentor you can rely on who knows how to build successful businesses and has a good model for doing so.

Wright

Knowing what you know now, what would you do differently if you could?

Hohnberger

I would have gone out on my own ten years earlier! I grew up in a very small town up in northeastern Wisconsin. My mom's dad owned the town grocery store, so she grew up in a family-owned business. My grandfather passed away before I was born so I never had the opportunity to meet him. My mom ran the store for several years, then sold it when she started having kids. She always told me to be an entrepreneur—to be in control of my own destiny—so it was always there inside. But I was fearful of taking the risk.

Looking back, if I could do it all over again, gosh, I would have taken my career and livelihood into my own hands from day one. If I had ten more years under my belt, *wow*, I can only imagine where I'd be today!

Wright

Where are you going from here? What's in the future for Craig Hohnberger?

Hohnberger

As I mentioned earlier, David, my vision is so much bigger today than it was when I first started. It incorporates both business and philanthropy and it's really exciting. I believe that to whom much is given, much is expected. And, I have been given a great opportunity and a lot of abilities so the least I can do is to take it is far as I can and give back as much as I can.

What we teach at ActionCOACH is a six-stage process on how to grow and develop your existing business to where it can work effectively without you. I'm actively in that process right now in my business. Once there, the advanced levels of the ActionCOACH systems are how to create long-term wealth and legacy building, through investing in and growing other businesses and real estate. Once my current business is through the six steps, I will then create a holding company to buy and build more businesses in other industries, all to fund charities, create future wealth, and help as many people as I can.

Right now I can only directly help the people who are a great fit for ActionCOACH. Indirectly, I can help their clients and families and the other people they influence, as well as give some advice to people who interview for ActionCOACH but who are not the right fit. I interview a lot of people in my recruitment office who are burnt out—they're frustrated in their current businesses or careers and they're treated like a number on a spreadsheet all too often anymore—so they are interested in joining ActionCOACH even though many really need to be in a different business.

So, ultimately, my goal is to leverage my ActionCOACH experiences—the sheer knowledge and skills, the network of people and the cash flow—to buy more businesses and grow them with the ActionCOACH systems. It'll be a lot of fun. And as I buy and build enough businesses across enough industries, no matter who I eventually meet, I'll be able to help them in their careers. Some will make great leaders of those companies and others will make great employees. If they've got career challenges and they're frustrated with their careers, we'll have an opportunity to put them into a business that's a better fit for them, as long as they are willing to play by our cultural rules of the game.

Wright

It sounds like you have a real passion for people getting into businesses and careers they are passionate about.

Hohnberger

I really do, David, because I see so many people who are on a career hamster-wheel unfortunately, and it's at all levels, from senior management on down.

I actually met a woman several weeks back who said there is a big difference at her job between the people who *"work on the carpet"* versus those who *"work on the concrete."* She works in a distribution facility. She said years ago, the executives would readily invite shop-floor workers to their homes for summer picnics and parties, but today executives would not be caught dead associating with them. She actually used that term—"the concrete versus the carpet." It's sad, David, that this is the way corporate America has become in so many cases, so I am out to change that.

I believe that to the extent we are not fully using and following the passions and gifts God gave us, we are not honoring Him. Unfortunately there are a lot of people in careers they chose long before they knew their real passions and gifts, and are now fearful of making a leap. That was me. I chose engineering and operations simply because my guidance counselors and academic ability suggested it might be a good fit. It really wasn't a great long-term fit and it took me years to figure that out. So, over time

I want to create as many bridges and opportunities as I can to help as many people as possible get to where they are most passionate and best suited career-wise and business-wise.

A significant portion of the revenues from these businesses will then be allocated to fund charities and other philanthropic opportunities to provide hand-ups for people who are less fortunate. I really have a passion for business ownership so I want to help less fortunate kids and other natural entrepreneurs, especially in our inner cities and in developing countries, to be able to create thriving businesses and provide more jobs and opportunities for those who live there. It'll never happen by myself, so I will obviously need to attract great people and great leaders to partner with me as we go down this path. So if you know any great people, David, please make an introduction.

Wright

Wow, Craig, I will certainly do that. This has been a great conversation. I'm really excited for you. It really sounds like Rose was a huge blessing to you, and that ActionCOACH has been a great move!

Hohnberger

It has been a very good move for me, David. It's changed my life. But I think the biggest part was doing that self-assessment up front. The advice I got from Rose on that airplane and the advice I got from my former boss, Mike and taking that to heart and really digging down was probably the most important thing I've ever done.

For others going through a similar type of career transition, they should be asking themselves the hard questions that will lead them to the right business or career for them. And they should be honest with themselves and not limit their goals or dreams. It is so freeing to have big dreams again.

Had I not had Rose and Mike in my life and not gone through the personal introspection I did, who knows where I would have ended up? I might very well have ended up owning a small chain of transmission shops! Nothing wrong with transmission shops for the right person, but it would certainly have not been the right business for me.

Wright

Craig, I appreciate all the time you've taken with me answering these questions. Thank you for your insightful answers. I've learned a lot just talking with you.

Hohnberger

Thank you, David. It has been my pleasure. Hopefully it will help someone gain some clarity for themselves. If I can help just one person make a great career decision and do it five or ten years faster than it took me, the impact will be well worth it. In fact, if anyone reading this or anyone you know, David, wants some free advice, all they have to do is contact me. I'll be glad to help in any way I can.

ABOUT CRAIG HOHNBERGER

Craig Hohnberger is an entrepreneur, speaker, and business coach. He owns a master franchise with ActionCOACH Business Coaching, the world's number one business coaching firm. He is passionate about making a difference in the world by inspiring people to achieve their goals and dreams through business and career transformation, and to use their success to pay it forward to others.

Craig Hohnberger
Oaktree Business Services of Ohio, LLC
dba ActionCOACH Business Coaching of
Indiana and Central/Southern Ohio
155 E. Columbus St., Suite 125
Pickerington, OH 43147
614.833.3211
www.CraigHohnberger.com

ROADMAP *to* SUCCESS 13

An interview with …

DR. THOMAS N. TAVANTZIS

David Wright (Wright)

Today we're speaking with Dr. Tavantzis, a licensed psychologist. He is President of Innovative Management Development (IMD) PC, a leadership and team consulting practice he founded in 1986. He also serves as Graduate Director of Training, Organizational Psychology, and Leadership programs at Saint Joseph's University in Philadelphia, Pennsylvania. His practical psychological experience of more than twenty-eight years includes executive and leadership roles in non-profits, faculty positions in several American and Greek universities, and for the past fifteen years, a leadership and team development consultant and an executive coach to leaders of nationwide and global companies.

Dr. Tavantzis' style in creating change is typically described as "creative, insightful, growth-producing, challenging, and supportive." During the course of his career he has published professional articles, book chapters, self-help articles, and training videos, as well as appearing on local television and radio talk shows. Dr. Tavantzis recently co-edited, *Don't Waste Your Talent,* which is in its second edition. It is a book that describes a strength-based methodology to personal and career development. Currently, Dr. Tavantzis is working on a new book based on his work developing new leaders.

Dr. Tavantzis, welcome to *Roadmap to Success*.

Thomas Tavantzis (Tavantzis)

Thank you, glad to be here.

Wright

So would you tell our readers a little bit about your focus on strengths in coaching and how you help individuals develop a road map to success?

Tavantzis

A fundamental idea for me is that having people understand, learn, and work from their strengths is the key for being able to contribute and be productive to an organization. Additionally, it is also being able to feel satisfied in what one is doing, and in that way it's a win-win for both the individual and for the organization.

However, unfortunately, for the most part, many people aren't aware of their strengths, they're more aware of their weaknesses, and even there, as Peter Drucker said, they are often wrong about what they don't do well. Many of the feedback systems that are in place with organizations don't really give people accurate feedback on what they do naturally and easily. The strength-based idea is getting people to understand, recognize, and use what they do easily and well. Frankly, it takes a lot more time, energy, and effort to remediate deficits in areas rather than having people move from a particular strength and then developing that strength to becoming excellent in an area.

Wright

It's strange that you're talking about people who don't recognize their strengths and weaknesses. I've been directing choral music for almost fifty years now, and you would be surprised at the number of people who sing in choirs, but who have no talent or aptitude for singing.

Tavantzis

Exactly. You'd be amazed at the number of people who are at the senior levels in organizations who really don't have a clear understanding of what they do well, and as a result they're not able to consciously focus in on their strengths. Interestingly, in not understanding one's own natural strengths one is also prevented from easily seeing how other people can best contribute on a team or in work roles.

Wright

In almost every leadership development workshop or seminar that I've attended, they almost invariably ask me to list my strengths and weaknesses. I'd be in really bad trouble if I didn't know what they are.

Tavantzis

Of course, we all learn to respond with the strengths and weaknesses we have learned about from others. What I am really talking about here is a more subtle and yet more basic level. Usually, when conducting a seminar, I ask people two questions: 1) what are the things that you do automatically and without having to think about when you first encounter a problem—how do you think? And, 2) what's your best contribution to a work team in the first five minutes?

Most people are at a loss because they're not really seeing what they are doing or how they process information automatically. These aren't big mysteries—people know somewhat, they just are not conscious of it, and therefore not able to use it purposefully in a situation. My focus is on moving hard-wired, automatic strengths into conscious awareness and purposeful use.

Wright

So how did you arrive at your present thinking model?

Tavantzis

I grew up in Athens, Greece, and had the fortunate experience of working with an American trained husband and wife team—a psychiatrist and a social psychologist at the Athenian Institute of Anthropos. They had both trained at the University of Chicago and returned to their homeland to develop their ideas in Greece. I became involved training with them when I was in college. With the Vassilious I participated in cross-cultural research, group, and family therapy and training, as well as in their work with leaders and organizations. I received early exposure and training before I knew much about anything in using systems thinking to understand people within organizations.

The particular way of approaching situations in our work was less to focus on people's pathology and weaknesses, but, rather, to focus on strengths and ask what skills they needed to develop to be more self-actualized, more competent. Our thinking focused on the premise that while one really can't do much about intelligence—that's fixed—one can help people develop their strengths, and one can certainly help people develop their social and emotional skills in how they interact, how they can be productive, useful, and how they impact others. Now I realize that we were teaching an early form of what is quite in vogue today and that is Emotional Intelligence.

Then when I was in my early twenties, I traveled with my Greek colleagues to different international conferences held in various places—Switzerland, Israel, Cyprus, and Yugoslavia—presenting papers on not only on our cross-culture research, but our work with groups and on what we were finding.

That early exposure to leaders in the field helped me because, when I returned to the United States to begin my doctoral studies, I ended up being able to work with two people who were also leaders in their fields. One is a fellow by the name of Walt Lifton, who is one of the originators of group-centered counseling, and another person, B. F. (Ted) Riess, was a psychoanalyst who also worked with organizations and leaders. From these two people I took what I had learned and went further in working with teams and individuals within organizations. For instance, in consulting, one approach was to study executives or teams in depth by videotaping their behavior in simulated situations, and then giving them feedback on what they were doing and what messages they were sending verbally and non-verbally. This was really a very micro approach to understanding individuals' strengths and building on them in real time.

I was also very involved with the family therapy movement in the late '60s and early '70s. At the time, family therapy represented a tremendous shift in thinking for psychotherapists. It was moving away from thinking about the individual as a container of problems and pathology to thinking that problems exist between people in a system. We needed to shift our thinking to how systems constrain behavior, therefore it made more sense to focus on skills and a search for strengths and not pathology. Now we learned a different question to ask when working with people—not what's wrong with them, but what strengths are they bringing to their situation, to their systems; what strengths do they possess that could be capitalized on to bring change?

It's always easier to shift people to doing more of what they're good at rather than trying to overcome and point out their weaknesses. When you start pointing out people's weaknesses, you don't really gain much. It's just much easier and more helpful to work with people from their strengths and move them further in that direction. Think of this as the difference between a deficit focus versus a strength focus and the reaction of the individual on the receiving end.

In my own small experiments with graduate students, they reported a deficit focus closing them off, increasing emotional withdrawal, and doubts about their worth and goals, while those who receive Positive or Strength-based feedback reports opened up to listening and feeling valued and quite motivated.

Wright

So how is this part of a larger paradigm shift?

Tavantzis

After the family therapy paradigm shift from person to system, some other shifts occurred as well and came along later. First, those of us in the field of psychology, about fifteen years ago, realized that we were overly focused on pathology in our training and research. Since then there has been a shift in focus toward something called positive psychology, which is about focusing on people, on values, on optimism, and on strengths.

Similarly, in the last decade, a new field has been developed called Positive Organizational Behavior. Several years ago the *Harvard Business Review* actually identified Positive Organizational Behavior as one of the ten big trends in one of their annual editions.

Much of this focus comes from the pioneering work of Peter Drucker, Daniel Goleman, Buckingham and Clifton, and others; they all reflect this paradigm shift in the sense of a focus on strengths. Peter Drucker was a major organizational thinker; he died several years ago. His thinking set the stage, probably thirty years ago, when he talked about Information workers, which is where the majority of the working people are at this point, and their need to know how they best contribute in the workplace. What's most important, according to Drucker, is being able to know how you can best contribute, how you can best learn quickly, what role(s) are you most satisfied in, and how you can contribute best to an organization.

Strength-based thinking has advanced more and more into the center of organizations, and you can see and hear it as you talk with people about what different companies are doing. The book I co-wrote that came out two years ago, *Don't Waste Your Talent,* is really about a methodology to help people develop the answers Drucker talked about as well as how to purposefully move their careers, based on information and data they have about themselves from a variety of resources, forward. It was also written to help individuals develop their own road map for success.

Wright

So how do you assist a person to arrive at understanding his or her strengths?

Tavantzis

I spent a considerable amount of time searching for that answer in the years after my graduate studies. At the time, I was consulting for a number of organizations and I was always looking for different and better individual and team scientific assessment instruments. That led me to quite a bit of research, as I spent about nine months looking at different instruments before I finally arrived at something that I think made sense. Most of the time, especially with some of the names of leaders I mentioned moments ago, people are helped to arrive at understanding their strengths based on one of two approaches: One approach uses a self-report, where you essentially vote for how you think you are. The famous self-report tool that many people have taken is the Myers-Briggs Type Inventory. The MBTI is a self-report because you essentially vote for how you think you are. However, a self-report is not a great source of data because it relies on you knowing yourself, and for the most part, many of us deceive ourselves quite a bit. Additionally, while a self-report does get to some important aspects, it is not a way to understand how we are hardwired to think and problem-solve.

The other main approach offered by people in our field is a 360-degree feedback, which is a multi-rater instrument. You rate yourself on certain kinds of traits, then you ask people who know you to rate you, and then you compare how you see yourself with how others see you. The critics of 360 surveys often describe it as not only an opinion poll, but a popularity contest too. Depending on how people feel about you they're going to rate you in certain ways. In and of themselves self-reports and 360s are not terrible approaches, as long as they are reliable and valid instruments; they're just not very good ways to get at your natural strengths. They instead get at your perceptions and other people's perceptions.

What I and others find is that the gold standard in psychometric testing is the use of work samples. A work sample is a timed test that isolates a particular cognitive trait. Let's say you want to understand how a person uses a particular way of problem solving. You would present him or her with a problem or puzzle that needs to be solved in a limited period of time. The person either possesses that ability and can solve the puzzle easily, or struggles. Time expires and that particular problem-solving ability might be revealed as not being a particular strength that the person has.

In the early nineties I found an instrument called The Highlands Ability Battery (THAB), which is based on measuring people on twenty-three different work samples. Each work sample measures a different natural strength or ability that we are "hard-wired" to use. What is revealed is how we naturally think, how we problem-solve, and what roles we seek out. The THAB is the foundation for my working with people in helping them look at their strengths. Instead of trial-and-error or having you "vote" for how you think you are, the Battery work samples reveal very clearly and objectively as to what are you hardwired to do easily.

Wright

Will you provide some examples of abilities that you measure?

Tavantzis

As I said, there are twenty-three that we measure (and probably more abilities that we have not yet figured out how to measure), but one of many that I find most interesting is something we call "Time Frame." A person is presented with a puzzle and we ask him or her to respond under the pressure of time in a particular way to a series of line drawings. Then from the responses, we look at the normative data of those who have also taken this work sample. We can then arrive at the person's percentile ranking.

What Time Frame purports to measure is one's natural way of thinking ahead. For instance, what's the distance between the time you make a decision and the time frame you can tolerate before you need to see a result? How far into the future do you think? Are you one of those people who can think five or seven years ahead? Not that you spend all your time there, but when something happens, you're able to look ahead into the implications of a decision.

People who score high in Time Frame—who have this as a strong ability as measured by this particular work sample—are people like CEOs of global companies, five-star generals, labor union negotiators, people who have to negotiate long-term contracts, people who seek out and do well in long-range planning and negotiations, and strategic thinkers in organizations. These types of people typically come out to be high in Time Frame.

Now, people who struggle with this work sample are more likely to be in what's called low or immediate time frame. They are like the "firemen" in an organization; it is almost as though they thrive in situations where they are asked to "put out fires." Give them a problem to solve, give them a project that is broken, and let them get on it, turn it around, and get immediate results; that's the key for Immediate Time Frame people. Typically, they're looking at a turnaround anywhere between three and nine months and so they are propelled by that sense of closure and the gratification of wrapping up and moving on.

Now, this doesn't mean to say that if you score low in Time Frame you can't think ahead. I've worked with engineers in plants and, almost uniformly, they're all immediate time frame. When I asked them about their job, they saw their job as "When the lights go out, our job is to put the lights back on." However, they also had to think about planned obsolescence of equipment, so that demanded that they spend some time thinking ahead. This is where skills come in versus abilities. Skills are what you've learned through experience and training, so they've learned to do planning, but it just wasn't as easy or as stress-free, and it didn't come as automatically as being driven for results in the immediate.

Wright

I wish I had talked to you before my daughter went into college last year.

Tavantzis

Recently, I received an e-mail from someone who had been part of a corporate program I conducted in 2003. His son had just turned sixteen and he recalled my saying that "the children can take the Ability Battery after fifteen." This man's son is sixteen and, as the father said, "I'd sure like him to take The Ability Battery because, as he comes up to thinking about his junior and senior year, it's going to help how he studies and how he thinks ahead." Across their lifespan people have found The

178

Highlands Ability Battery useful when it comes to making decisions about roles, tasks, and work environments.

Another ability we measure is called "Classification." Now, this is a fast-paced, problem-solving ability. If people score strongly in this they need to be in roles that call for fast-paced decision-making.

Here is how it works: people are presented with a series of seven pictures, and they have to pick three that have something to do with each other. Sounds easy, doesn't it? However, the work sample is composed of nineteen increasingly complex problems and less time to solve them. A person who has this ability can look at how unrelated facts go together quickly and can solve problems without a lot of information. We are really measuring inductive problem solving and decision-making where one takes disparate information and pulls it together quickly to conclusion.

People who score high in Classification are typically drawn to roles or environments that are very chaotic, unstructured, and where they're being asked to solve problems—novel problems—on a regular basis; that is exhilarating for them. Typically, people who score high in Classification would be drawn to work where new and novel problems come at them rapidly (e.g., trial attorneys or emergency room physicians).

For example, when you go to see your doctor you want to give him or her a constellation of symptoms and you want a tentative diagnosis quickly. You don't really want the doctor to say, "Well, okay, why don't you come back next week? Let me think about it and I'll get back to you." One expects to be given a diagnosis, if at all possible, while in the doctor's office. That's an example of a role where having high classification is helpful.

Now, while scoring high in Classification sounds great and everybody might like to have that ability, on the other hand, in large corporate environments when you're in a leadership role, being that kind of fast-paced problem-solver is not necessarily a good trait for a leader. The person who scores high in Classification really thrives on being the sole decision-maker. The person is an expert in diagnosing the problem and then wants to move quickly on to another problem. Most decisions in large organizations are not made by the solo trouble-shooter—there is not usually a need for decisions to be made in this quick fashion. Problem solving is really done through teams, discussion, and collaboration. In fact, an important point is that high scores on this ability battery don't necessarily mean that you can function in all roles—sometimes your higher abilities can be more challenging in a role where lower abilities, as in our example of Classification, may work better.

To continue with this example, people who score low in Classification have a different way of problem solving. When I describe it you'll see that it makes more sense in terms of executive leadership for someone to be lower in Classification. People who score lower in Classification are more about gathering information. They are better able to listen to what people are saying because they are not rushing to solve a problem. They seek out information from others when they're faced with a novel problem.

For the most part people who have been experienced in a role, such as a manager for ten or fifteen years, thrive because they are seeing problems in the present and then they can compare what is coming in with past experiences that they've had. They can apply past experiences to solve current problems.

People who score low in Classification are intuitive. They can be very fast-paced but it's derived from a different way of decision-making and problem solving. We know from one study of executives leading nationwide firms and from our experience that people who are typically in major leadership roles are more likely to score low in Classification or are problem-solvers who use their past experiences versus the fast-paced, diagnostic problem-solvers.

Again, we measure twenty-three different abilities in all with the Battery.

Another set of crucial abilities we measure are Learning Channels. We measure five Learning Channels:

1. Designs and pictures and graphs (Design Memory)
2. Reading recall (Verbal Memory)
3. Listening (Tonal Memory)
4. Movement (Kinesthetic Memory)
5. Numbers, and trivia and data (Number Memory)

Knowing your learning channels is significant in order to understand your easiest and quickest way of taking in new information. For example, do you learn easiest through reading (e.g., if you read something, does that stick in your head?)? Perhaps you learn easily through listening (e.g., you hear a conversation and then recall it six months later when you run into a client again, and you relate the story he or she told you about his or her kids, and now you instantly connect).

Wright

Most of the folks I talk to who are sales trainers are auditory learners.

Tavantzis

Exactly—the learning channels aren't new but how we measure them is different since we use work samples. We actually use music tests to measure some of the learning channels. These tests were developed by a psychologist, Charlie Seashore, to be used for identifying musical talent in young children. There are other resources that suggest that these same tests are related to ways you learn.

People who have high kinesthetic memory not only have trouble sitting still; they have lots of energy and they learn through doing—hands-on experience—and they take notes when they're listening to something. Of course, by taking notes they're bringing it into their brain in another way, and when they're with people they can pick up more on nonverbal behavior because they are attuned to physical movement.

My own personal theory of why I'm a terrible golfer is a result of my very low rhythm memory. If you're an athlete, rhythm memory is about your body remembering muscle movement through time, and so you can repeat the same movement over and over again, rather than reinventing that movement. It is almost as though I have to reinvent my golf swing every time I get on a tee because my body has difficulty with remembering muscle movement.

However, it's not just about abilities when we're looking at strengths from the perspective of Positive Organizational Behavior. I'm not one for reducing someone down to one factor (i.e., you are only your abilities). Both common sense and research suggest that we as people are more complex than that. In fact, over the past sixty years there seems to be a consensus in the literature that there are eight factors that go into personal effectiveness, and abilities are just one factor, although it is a fundamental one.

Wright

Would you go through the eight-factor model?

Tavantzis

First, it is helpful for people consider where they are in their career and how they arrived at the current role; this is the *Career Development Factor*. Here we are providing an opportunity for clients to examine their stage of career development and whether they are at a Turning Point or a Building Stage.

A Turning Point is when people find answers they gave to some of life's basic questions (e.g., how to do I balance work and family? How do I contribute? Am I satisfied?).

A Building Stage is when you have chosen a path and spend time and energy developing skills and competencies. However, life can throw you curveballs and suddenly you find yourself thrown from a Building Stage to a Turning point through company downsizing.

Another factor is *Skills*. Here we are looking at what skills people have learned to date. Skills and abilities are different. For example, let's say you have high rhythm ability. Just because you're naturally coordinated, have lots of energy, and can learn through muscle movement easily doesn't make you a good tennis player. You still have to practice and develop the skills. However, it will be easier to acquire the skills because of your natural ability in that area. Thus, skills can be ways to expand your abilities. We can also develop skills to compensate for low abilities in certain areas; people do that too.

Another factor is *Interests*. We often hear "do what you love," so in this factor we examine what excites you, what fascinates you, what are you passionate about in your life? Your Interests are a source of energy and creativity. This is another major component in helping people think about their careers and be successful.

Personal Style is another factor and here we are seeking what work environment pulls you personality-wise. We look at several personality dimensions including the continuum of introversion-extroversion. Some of the questions we ask here are: What kind of interpersonal work environment comes easy to you? What kind of roles do you seek out? Do you seek out roles where you can work through and with other people in a team-oriented approach or do you seek out a role where you can learn something and lead through your expertise? How you "do" these roles will be influenced by whether you're more in the introverted or in the extroverted world. People lead most easily based on what their Personal Style is; however, leaders adapt and need to learn how they can become stressed by temporarily moving into another style.

Just to reiterate, so far I have outlined five of the eight factors: *Abilities, Career Development Stage, Skills, Interests,* and *Personal Style*. Another of the eight factors we also look at is *Family of Origin*. We are not interested in the family dysfunction that each of us brings from our family; but rather, the work roles learned. Essentially, what did your family teach you about the world of work before your brain was fully formed? This usually occurs around eight years old. Early on you form impressions about the world of work. You get ideas about how work and daily stress is handled by the big people in your life—the people you depend on. You are not able to articulate these insights, but they are certainly coming in as information for you and they form your mental model of the world and work relationships.

People in the work environment, especially when their perception of stress increases, tend to approach the workplace as a reflection of their own family of origin and unconsciously use coping mechanisms based on these same earlier perceptions. For example, we see people jockey for the position of being a "favorite sibling" or dealing with present day authorities based on how they dealt with authorities from their past.

The Family of Origin piece is significant because, in our individual coaching work and in our corporate workshops, we are assisting people in looking at what messages have been communicated and passed down over the generations within their family. We find for many it's almost an awakening to the fact that their family's history has influenced who they are becoming in ways they usually are unaware. For instance, routinely the following questions emerge: What has been the role of women in my family over three generations? What are the messages I live by? What was passed on from my family as a philosophy about work? Our goal is to try to pick up on these themes, to understand them, and assist you in understanding how they impact you as a leader, as a team member, and as a worker.

And briefly, the last two factors of this model are *Values and Goals*. Values are quite significant because we ask what people stand for as they move into the future. Are you able to articulate your values? Are you living your values? A related key question is what values do other people see you living? And lastly, putting it together, we ask people to examine and develop their short- and long-term goals.

Once we have worked through the eight factors, the next phase of the work is even more critical because now we move into integrating all this information into a new and different narrative for the people creating a Personal Vision, thus providing them with a blueprint or road map to success.

Wright

To whom have you applied your methods?

Tavantzis

Over the past fifteen years I have applied these methods to a variety of groups. As the Director of Organizational Psychology and Leadership at St. Joseph's University, in Philadelphia, Pennsylvania, I direct two programs, one for evening classes for adults seeking to complete this undergraduate degree, and the second program is the Graduate program in Organizational Development, Psychology, and Leadership. Among other courses, I teach career development courses in both programs.

In the Undergraduate courses we can have students who range in age from twenty-five to sixty. Our graduate students are typically part-time students with considerable years of experience in the working world and have arrived at a certain point in their careers where they want (and in some cases need) to come back for their master's degree. I am fortunate because I also get to work with these very experienced people in training and development, management, HR people who are already working within organizations. In both of those different groups I've been teaching a course called "Career and Personal Development," which is based on the method I described. Essentially, I use an experiential approach to teaching about career development and how you work with people as a career coach using this eight-factor model. The university setting has offered me an excellent place to test out my ideas over the past years and get feedback from my adult students.

Most of my work, however, consists of individuals who seek me out in my private coaching and consulting practice. These are adults in transition—college students, graduate students, and some high school students—much like the example I gave earlier. Over the last fifteen years, my passion for this work really comes out in my main life work applying this model within a variety of industries—pharmaceuticals, energy, technical, engineering, and communications.

Wright

Do you have any success examples?

Tavantzis

A very recent example comes to mind. I was engaged by a scientist who was also a Senior Vice-President (SVP). His challenge, and the basis of the engagement, was to reduce the significant conflict that existed within his department among the managers while assisting them in developing a vision for themselves within the company so they could emerge as leaders who were "initiators" rather than "reactors."

My approach was to first work with him individually, going through the eight factors, coming up with a model for him of his leadership style, which meant being able to look at how he led and what role(s) he could contribute from.

As we went through the individual coaching process he realized that he had to rethink how he organized his department! He was under the mistaken impression that as a manager, leader, and director, he should be the center of all things and all decisions, which was extremely stressful for him. However, that's how he was trying to hold the department together. An alternative model emerged from the results of the Ability Battery and from understanding the impacts of the other factors. An approach that would work better for him and build on his considerable talents because of the kinds of abilities he had and family background as well as values, was to form and understand the people in his team who were the more senior people and who had abilities that complemented his. Instead of trying to "do it all" and thinking that if he didn't do it all he was a failure, his main task became to convene a small group of people, give them the current problem, and ask for a discussion. His job as manager, leader, and director was really to pick the best answer, the best idea, or the best solution, and then work it through the corporate bureaucracy. This was much more consistent with his natural abilities of being able to focus and drive for results and keep a long-term vision in mind. As he shifted his role and saw positive results, he then brought me in to successfully work with the rest of the team.

I ended up working with that group for six months. Over time the conflict was replaced by teamwork and collaboration. I spoke with the SVP a year later, and what he said was quite remarkable. Apparently, immediately after I left, the company started going through a merger. Many of them would lose their jobs, and conflicts throughout the whole company intensified. People were acting out their anger all over the place. They would more frequently call in sick and there was vandalism because people were angry. What this SVP was able to see during that more chaotic time was that his department was actually one of the better functioning departments in the whole organization because they were helping each other figure out the transition rather than competing with each other or withdrawing and being angry about what was happening. To me this is a significant intervention that worked and helped these folks out.

Another global company I had been working with for several years was being taken over by a British company. Many of the executives I had worked with didn't know what their next step was going to be—either they would be offered a position in the new company or not. If offered a position they would either take it or not, which might mean relocation for them and their family. They brought me in based on the past relationship I had established with people. We were able to work with mostly VPs in Germany.

I think there was one American among the twenty-seven people who were in the room, and we worked over three days in helping each of these people develop a career plan. It involved doing career coaching in a group intensively for three days. These folks worked very hard—sometimes twelve-hour days—to come up with individual plans. We asked each of them to look ahead in their careers, while also helping them to manage this continuing transition, which they were finding incredibly stressful. For many of the participants this kind of downsizing was a completely novel experience, especially in Germany and in France, because it was unheard of. Downsizing for them was more of a recent American import that we gave to Europe. They were not used to having to deal with this kind of sudden and major life and career transition.

For us this was a very different audience and a unique experience at that point of our work. It's been over seven years ago and I'm still in touch with many of them—they contact me periodically. They all saw this experience as one of the major highlights and successes for themselves in their career, and we felt the same.

There are many other successes I could point to but these are the ones that stand out as turning points for us in our approach. More recent successes include a summer Career and Personal Development graduate course I am teaching right now. The students in their Reflection Journals routinely describe this course as the "single most important developmental experience in their career." Their excitement for their journey is palpable. We recently completed a pilot program for twenty-eight IT employees from an energy company that we created to assist their employees in planning and managing their careers. The evaluations of the pilot were so positive that this program will be rolled out immediately across the enterprise.

Wright

So switching gear for a minute, would you tell me more about how you approach coaching with individuals and how you help them in developing a road map for success?

Tavantzis

I think one first needs to consider the difference between someone who is a trained psychologist versus someone who comes at coaching from an MBA perspective. I would argue that someone who has been initially trained in in-depth counseling and psychotherapy is going to bring a greater level of awareness and sophistication to understanding the coaching relationship and the how of developing a road map for success for a person. That person is better able to actively listen to an issue at multiple levels and can then decide with the client where to focus in the here and now and where to focus on the future. A trained counseling professional will bring an empathetic understanding of the different ways people struggle with change and how they both defend themselves and maintain the status quo while wanting to grow.

As we know, most people, even though they might say to the contrary, are really reluctant to embrace change because it's filled with ambiguity and uncertainty. In fact, the implicit message people often send is less about changing themselves and more about how others should change! Being empathic and supportive are critical pre-conditions in helping a person look at what his or her next step is and what the person needs to do. Additionally, people need to find out how to move past embracing behaviors and attitudes that aren't working. At the same time they need to at least feel safe and secure and move to the uncertainty of something new that they're not really convinced will make a difference.

And why should they be convinced? Change is a difficult step. It's like walking into a dark room and not knowing where the furniture is located and stumbling around. Your task as a coach is to guide and to help the client make that transition from the comfort of knowing to the discomfort of not knowing exactly the placement of all the pieces in the room. And when we think of this transition, what we mean is trying to have people see the gap between what they would like to be, and what they'd like to do, and where they are now. Our goal is to help them move past that discrepancy through focusing on their strengths. For me, I think it is clearly about having people rewrite the stories—their life narratives—by going through each of the eight factors, collecting data about themselves, and enabling them to discuss their data with other people (not just with me) in a supportive workshop format or a group or one-to-one relationship.

In coaching you're changing people's narratives about themselves. All of a sudden the narrative that they have, which might be a narrow narrative based on their family of origin or the feedback they've gotten from others over the years, must be changed. Their narrative might also be something like, "I'm this kind of person." Suddenly, their narrative is expanded into, "I'm also this kind of person, as well as this other person, and I have these interests and these strengths," and so on. By being able to move clients to a richer narrative about what they tell themselves, we move beyond the constraints of those earlier years and the limited views about what they can do.

Again, one needs to have the clinical sensibility to recognize this is hard personal work, fraught with risks.

Consider this: we're all engaged and involved within systems, either with our families or our friends; it's hard if we start to change because that pushes our system out of balance. As a result, there are system forces at work that constrain people from changing. For example, in a work setting you really have to intervene, not only with the person who is the client, but also with the person's work team. One needs to recognize and answer the question: just because a person is willing to start trying something new, is the team able to make changes in how they are viewing this person?

It is similar when working outside of an organization when an adult is the one who wants to change work and career but his or her change is going to impact what the spouse and children are doing. Is the family prepared? Have they been prepared? Has anyone prepared them for what change means to all of them? Will the family support the change? Will friends support the change? These are critical questions that need to be answered within the coaching relationship.

Again, when we speak of changing the networks we are embedded in, our work, family, and friends are involved. Our systems are not maliciously "doing it to us." But systems by their nature do constrain us from changing.

One mechanical system example is, for instance, when you want to change the temperature on your household thermostat, no matter what you try, the temperature range that kicks off the furnace stays the same until you reset the thermostat. Therefore, to "reset the system," good coaching involves not just working with the person, but also working with the system in which he or she is embedded.

In my work there is quite an emphasis on role-play and practicing new behaviors, as well as considerable homework. My expectation is that clients will make a commitment of time and energy. They have to do homework and they have to go out and interview people. We ask people to be quite active; it's not just reflecting and it's not just counting on me to come up with solutions—they have to generate information and data about themselves and about their world so they can start finding different connections for a new narrative and creation of a personal vision.

Wright

So why do leaders need to understand themselves?

Tavantzis

The road to success for a leader is about being someone who can move others into a direction or activity that is in their collective best interest. To me this suggests that the leader has to be communicative, knowledgeable, and collaborative with others. In a sense, leaders have to be able to take on at least three different roles: 1) head of the team, essentially saying, "Okay folks, follow me; let's go make it happen," 2) at another time they're part—they're members—of the team, and 3) they should be able to pick up on the collective dynamics of the team and follow leaders they are creating on the team.

For me, this is a more flexible way of thinking about leadership. We know from Jim Collins' research that leaders don't have to be the larger than life charismatic voices people are going to be thrilled and swayed by; no, actually you don't want that. What you want are leaders who help people think and use their ability to be innovative, to contribute, and who require a leader who has a enough sense to get out of the way sometimes and follow what they've supported creating.

To be able to contribute as a leader from this view, a leader or someone who aspires to be a leader, needs to know what he or she can contribute. Instead of thinking that leaders can do everything, they need to find out what their best contribution is. They need to determine the areas in which they need assistance from others, and who complements them in different ways. Another question would be what their stimulus value as a leader is—when they're talking, what happens to people around them? Do people want to get involved at that point, or are they being turned off? Leading is not just being authoritative and having a job title; it's also mutual respect and strength-based acknowledge of the people around you—those you are asking to work with you. By knowing themselves, leaders model the way for their organization, as eventually all leaders are scrutinized by their deeds and not by their words.

Wright

It's very interesting for me to learn that you believe leaders become increasingly more isolated from feedback. In my company, I used to hold all the meetings, now I've got divisions holding their own meetings, and I don't get feedback as quickly; sometimes I don't get feedback at all.

Tavantzis

Yes, of course—who is going to tell the "emperor" she or he "has no clothes on"? Information doesn't flow up the hierarchy very easily. I think that's where a reliable coach helps leaders—by helping them take a look in the mirror in a way that they are most likely not doing.

Wright

I seem to get a lot more interpreted feedback than I do raw feedback nowadays.

Tavantzis

Yes, feedback all too frequently becomes filtered and cleansed when delivered upward. There is no question that reality checks work for leaders.

Recently, at a conference for bio-pharmaceutical executives of small- to mid-sized companies I was stunned to hear one executive note that one significant issue for him in trying to get his business to go from just a start-up to a mid-sized pharmaceutical company was the time he takes to understand himself. That was a beacon of hope there, because the other CEOs on the panel looked at him with astonishment as if to say, "What are you talking about? Oh, you're talking about self-understanding. Yes, that's good, let's get back to business—" What this CEO was describing was a great example of knowing full well that he'll be increasingly isolated from feedback; he's trying to build up ways to get unfiltered information.

We all have our blind spots, however, they become magnified when we're in a leadership role. And, consider this, if we combine the blind spots that we already have with the decrease in feedback, we have a recipe for what we see in corporations that have been in the media—CEOs who think they can do just about anything and that they are immune and impervious.

Of course, what I am saying also pertains to potential leaders. When I consider the larger picture I am really looking at how to help employees—from the top to the bottom—to understand their careers, their strengths, and how they can be involved to maximize their own satisfaction and their own contribution; that's the win-win.

On a practical level, what I do these days (and the coaching is a piece of it) is work with companies to install end-to-end solutions to talent development and succession planning challenges and issues. I also help companies develop their competency models in a cost-effective manner. As an organizational psychologist/consultant, I assist leaders who want to focus on developing their organizational talent systems and then align that to different assessment tools so that there is a seamlessness to the process—from selection to hiring to development to employee appraisals that are built in—helping their people develop in a strength-based way.

Wright

It sounds as though you're thinking larger than just coaching leaders.

Tavantzis

Right. For me, my work is coming full circle and back to my initial training in systems thinking in Athens, Greece. My own initial training and thinking was itself greatly influenced by the systemic view originally inspired by the ancient Greeks and the Hellenic world. Thinking and acting from a systems point of view in a coaching relationship means understanding their context and creating interventions that can shift entire groups. To do that effectively, first one needs to have the leaders on board and then work through the whole organization. For me here lies a much greater sense of accomplishment; it is also more meaningful to me—I feel I can be useful to an organization and its people. My larger mission is about helping organizations develop their people by providing road maps to be successful both within and outside the organization.

Wright

What a great conversation, Dr. Tavantzis. I think I've been through an Advanced Graduate Psychology course today. It's very, very interesting. You've given me a lot to think about. It sounds like you've come up with some great ways of helping leaders and individuals in developing their road maps for success!

Tavantzis

Yes, and thank you for your kind words.

Wright

Today we've been talking with Thomas Tavantzis, PhD. A licensed psychologist, Dr. Tavantzis is President of Innovative Management Development (IMD), a leadership team consulting practice that he founded back in 1986. People talk about him as being creative, insightful, growth producing, challenging, and supportive. I don't know about you, but I agree with all of that.

Thank you so much, Dr. Tavantzis, for being with us today on *Roadmap to Success.*

Tavantzis

Thank you.

About Thomas Tavantzis

Dr. Thomas Tavantzis is a licensed psychologist who specializes in people development. He is President of Innovative Management Development (IMD) PC, a leadership and team consulting practice he and his wife founded in 1986. He also serves as Graduate Director of Training, Organizational Psychology, and Leadership programs at St. Joseph University in Philadelphia, Pennsylvania. His practical psychological experience of more than twenty-eight years includes executive and leadership roles in non-profits, faculty  positions in several American and Greek universities, and for the past fifteen years, a leadership and team development consultant and an executive coach to leaders of nationwide and global companies.

Dr. Tavantzis' style in creating change is typically described as "creative, insightful, growth-producing, challenging, and supportive." During the course of his career he has published professional articles, book chapters, self-help articles, and training videos, as well as appearing on local television and radio talk shows. Dr. Tavantzis recently co-edited, *Don't Waste Your Talent,* which is in its second edition. It is a book that describes a strength-based methodology to personal and career development. Currently, Dr. Tavantzis is working on a new book based on his work developing new leaders.

Dr. Thomas N. Tavantzis
IMD
568 West Valley Rd
Wayne, Pa 19087
Thomas.tavantzis@gmail.com
www.IMDleadership.com

ROADMAP *to* SUCCESS 14

An interview with ...

JO ANNE BISHOP

David Wright (Wright)

Today we're talking with JoAnne Bishop, PhD, Founder and CEO of Crossing Bridges & Associates, a coaching, consulting, and conflict mediation firm located in Honolulu, Hawaii. She is a motivational speaker, author, Certified Professional Coach, and Certified Hypnotherapist. JoAnne reaches an international client base including CEOs, entrepreneurs, senior executives, and top sales producers. Specializing in one-on-one coaching, conflict mediation, and corporate training, she has co-authored *Success Strategies: The High Achiever's Guide to Success* and *Success is a State of Mind*. She holds graduate degrees in Counseling Psychology and Public Policy Administration and has appeared on television and radio.

Dr. Bishop, welcome to *Roadmap to Success*.

Jo Anne Bishop (Bishop)

Thank you, David; it is a pleasure to be here.

Wright

So in your view does success require a road map?

Bishop

Yes, in my view, a road map is an important tool in creating success. It is an essential ingredient as a means of navigation in every journey. I don't believe that all successful people decide consciously on a plan; rather, that their destination to success is based upon unconscious impressions from within that takes them in one direction or another. The percentage of individuals who can use this method is much smaller than those who use a more consciously delineated plan, because this structure provides direction and can conserve energy and time. The direct and indirect route is traveled through daily decision-making. Often, with the indirect route, it's not until people look back over their life that they actually see the path they have followed emerge.

Whether it's a conscious or unconscious road to success, there are four specific components that guide will us. Vision, specific intention, commitment to action, and passion will move us toward our destination. Passion and commitment are emotionally based products of the brain's right hemisphere. Determination, direction, and decision-making are products of the brain's left hemisphere and encompass specific intention. Integration of the power of both of the brain's hemispheres combines to access our unlimited potential.

It's my belief that we need an integrated force of mind, body, and spirit to effectively move forward. In this process, self-direction is a leadership skill. The most important part of any journey is consciously taking the first step. This enables us to use all of our inherent leadership skills to move forward. Our leadership ability is enhanced when we take risks and learn from our experience. Self-direction is an integral part of a successful life and is a byproduct of leadership.

People can be taught to be self-directed. In addition, life's circumstances, experience, family systems, and adversity can evoke inherent leadership abilities. People can become self-directed through training. Professional training enables people to utilize talents that are specific and unique to them. These qualities are developed through self-exploration, knowledge, intelligence (both intellectual and emotional), curiosity, and the willingness to succeed. The ability to take risks and move beyond safety zones increases our self-trust and self-worth.

Adversity is sometimes a required impetus that allows individuals to rise to the occasion when life challenges them. Adversity in corporations, organizations, and governments often leads to a reorganization process that creates chaos in the workplace. Chaos precedes creativity and problem solving in many instances. Chaos can be seen as adversity because it takes us into unknown territory. Chaos breaks apart stagnant situations that can force us into action.

A road map that utilizes a direct route is a strategic, structured plan that incorporates incremental planning. It can be measured by factual data, benchmarks, and quantitative methods. Many times, the road we start is not the one we finish because of obstacles and roadblocks that have rerouted our paths. These roadblocks are challenges that help us reconsider options and provide time to pause, rethink, and reconsider our routes. Self-direction then becomes an opportunity to trust that obstacles or challenges may be in our best interest even if they bring adversity and chaos with them.

As I said earlier, it is not necessarily what the road looks like, but how we travel the road. Leadership activates the commitment to begin. We take action based upon on our intention to succeed, which in turn sets off a chain of events. The events create probable realities and future outcomes that would not have been available before making the commitment. Starting on any road to success is the intention to succeed, which creates a flow of energy opening doors that would have not been there without infusing our intention with passion, vision, and determination.

I've always believed in the saying that when a student is ready the teacher appears. Being ready means having the desire and intention for change. A teacher can be a mentor, friend, an opportunity, or an obstacle that will guide and challenge us to stay on the roadway or reconsider and reevaluate our direction. In my experience, help or support is always there when we have the courage to begin.

Wright

You use signposts as indicators. What does that mean?

Bishop

Signposts are signals or indicators that either verify we are going in the right direction or guide us to make a change to the chosen path. Signposts can be equated to landmarks.

Mentors, obstacles, or events can help lead us to the next step in the process. By learning to observe obstacles as signposts, we can release resistance to change. This can be a valuable opportunity to learn and grow instead of blaming ourselves or becoming victims of the obstacle.

Signposts, like opportunities, can provide courage to change directions. This is not always an easy process. It may appear that we are making false starts by changing direction or viewing the initial goal as inappropriate. Even if we have to begin anew, giving ourselves permission to see life and the direction that we are taking as a process, instead of a series of wins or losses, can lead to an experience that may be a turning point in our lives.

A client of mine calls this process "testing his metal." He believes that through these challenges and experiences he grows in self-regard and self-trust; both are attributes of a leader. It's all in our attitude. We learn to evaluate the signposts that tell us if we're headed in the best direction. This is a valuable tool on the road to success. There is a Buddhist saying, "If a wise man loses his way, he will go back to the beginning of his path instead of wondering in circles." In other words, it takes wisdom and courage to admit you are going the wrong way, identify the signposts and begin again.

Wright

Are some people just lucky or do they really have to design a structured plan to be successful?

Bishop

Seneca, a first century Roman philosopher stated, "Luck is what happens when preparation meets opportunity." This describes my outlook on this question. It's important to distinguish between being lucky and being open to opportunity.

Sidney Poitier provided a good example of this philosophy during a recent interview on *Larry King Live*. He inferred his belief that each individual makes a thousand little decisions in his or her lifetime that lead to Providence giving a hand on each person's pathways. He went on to explain how he got into acting.

One day he was led to an audition for a small role in a play. The director asked him to leave the audition because he couldn't read the script. He had hidden his illiteracy from the world until that moment. He left the audition determined to learn to read. He stated that at that moment he unconsciously chose his destiny.

Providence or luck has many faces, not all benevolent. The director provided an opportunity for him to change. Mr. Poitier chose not to be victimized by the experience, but to be challenged. His willingness to be accountable for the skills he didn't possess created a turning point that put him on the road to stardom. He had to do the groundwork, which meant that he would be challenged with hardship, sacrifice, and self-doubt. The experience with the director clarified what he did want to do and he was willing to do what was necessary to acquire success.

When opportunities present themselves, foresight and courage are needed to recognize them. Luck or Providence is what we bring to ourselves based upon the many decisions we make and our attitudes. Each decision is part of the road map that can change our lives, opening up a myriad of possibilities.

Leadership qualities enable individuals to carve out their destinies through proactive living. The decisions that we make every day create a structured plan, even if in the moment we aren't consciously aware we are creating that structure.

Wright

So what part does destiny play in success?

Bishop

Destiny can be defined in two ways. One definition comes from the Middle English word meaning fate. The second definition comes from a Latin derivative, *destinata,* which means to make firm or establish. We can live our lives based upon how external circumstances affect us, which is a belief in fate, or we can direct our destiny by our desire to influence our lives through proactive decision-making that outlines our intentions to succeed.

Self-direction influences the decisions that we make. My definition of destiny is the use of my free will and leadership ability to influence the events and successes in my life. I must accept the challenges that are presented to me, move through them, or release what I cannot change and let Providence play its part. Therefore, I am a co-creator of my destiny and responsible for the creation of my future.

Wright

You emphasize the need for developing the intuitive or creative mind to enhance decision-making. Would you tell our readers how that would help?

Bishop

Creative and intuitive decision-making occurs naturally for some people, others have to learn to harness this skill.

The process becomes distinctive when it influences decision-making that moves against the tide of a current market or a consensus of a general population. The intuitive/creative mind has provided the world with innovative products, services, philosophies, and technological change; it's also provided scientific discoveries that have increased the quality of life. The intuitive/creative process has evolved. I think it's important to say that education of every kind is the vessel that allows the creative mind to emerge. Education allows us to utilize experience and knowledge to enhance a rational, disciplined, and logical mind, which is the foundation required to make sense of creative and intuitive impressions. It will also prepare us to meet opposition when new ideas rock the boat of traditionally held beliefs. We only have to look at Galileo or the Civil Rights Movement to see what the intuitive/creative process evokes.

In a recent graduation address at the University of Southern California Medical School, the keynote speaker indicated to the graduates that the current medical knowledge they had gained would be obsolete in ten years. He based his conclusion upon the pace of new development of research in medicine and biology. Although obsolescence is inevitable, he believed that the academic processes the graduates had mastered were the necessary foundation for the scientific breakthroughs of the future. Their education had provided them with the necessary skills to hone their minds, acquire knowledge, analyze, research, and chose methods of action to solve future scientific challenges.

We must understand that in any field, groundwork is the necessary foundation for all intuitive creative inspiration. We all have to pay our dues in one way or another. This applies to personal, executive, and organizational decision-making. We have to have the ability to ask the right questions, risk opposition, be curious, and not satisfied with the status quo. The intuitive mind requires this process to connect non-sequential information in a variety of innovative ways. Our evolution as a society would have required a much greater time period without the intuitive inspirations of many contributors. The intuitive mind catapults us toward new ideas. The rational mind provides the discipline and analysis to find ways to put these ideas into action.

We can see this in the global marketplace. Companies such as Facebook, Google, Apple, and Virgin Atlantic Airlines value intuitive decision-making. They encourage their employees to utilize creative talents to understand the heartbeat of a potential market long before the rest of their industries. This propels the company into a leadership position. The intuitive, innovative thought process is later integrated into the company's decision-making model.

It is important for each of us to recognize that our intuitive impressions are valid and uniquely individualized. We can recognize these impressions through an orderly developmental process. This can be accomplished by taking time each day to clear our minds, meditate, self-reflect, journal, read, and research. All of these approaches stimulate the intuitive/creative mind. Practice of any skill can be nurtured to mastery. Intuitive decision-making is a skill that can be learned through daily application.

Wright

So what can people do to effectively get through roadblocks?

Bishop

We each have the opportunity to synthesize our life experience in a positive way and choose a philosophical orientation that pursues the development of our individual talents. When facing roadblocks, a mentor, coach, psychotherapist, or trainer can provide the opportunity for objective feedback that stimulates the creative/intuitive process. This orientation encompasses the notion that we don't have to meet challenges alone.

I feel that overcoming many challenges can be so great that it can temporarily immobilize us. Change creates fear. Fear is universally instinctual when associated with risk. Understanding that our fear can promote action enables us to transform the fear into intuitive/creative power. We must give ourselves permission to acknowledge the fear. We can transform the fear to overcome obstacles. It's also important to recognize when we need to seek outside support to expedite the process if necessary.

This is what I recommend to my clients when faced with roadblocks:

- Take a step back from the challenge.
- Understand that fear is a natural reaction and a byproduct of our willingness to risk.
- Learn to use fear creatively by harnessing the energy created by fear in a positive manner through affirmation and action.
- Imagine and affirm the desired outcome.
- Be willing to release the known for the unknown.

- Define, on paper, what possible solutions are available (writing is one of the best ways of integrating the right and left brain hemispheres for problem-solving).
- Reevaluate the challenge, choose a solution, and take action. This process may have to be repeated several times.
- After thought, we might find the challenge insurmountable, which is part of the release process.
- Be willing to release the insurmountable challenge and develop a new plan.
- Start again.
- Never give up on your dreams.

One of the most important gifts we can give ourselves is the time to respond to a challenge instead reacting to it. Sleeping on a problem has been scientifically proven to increase analytical ability. Sleep enhances our mental acuity and gives the subconscious mind time to work on the problem. If the obstacle remains after using the tools I have provided, it might require abandoning the current course and starting anew. David, many of the contributors to your books have said this in a variety of ways.

To simply this concept, I've developed a process with the acronym EASY:

Envision victory,
Affirm the outcome,
Start the process, and realize that
You have the answers within you.

Trust in yourself.

Wright

You said you believe that an individual's road map can affect the world community. Will you tell our readers what you mean by that?

Bishop

Yes, I will. David, I feel that you're a good example of an individual's road map affecting the world community. By starting your company you have: gathered a team, a product, people of influence in the human development field, nurtured emerging leaders through your training programs, and provided a platform for the experts to present their ideas to many people. The risk that you have taken to start your company has resulted in changing the lives of people who read the books that you publish; you had a vision and you took a risk.

Many people, such as Walt Disney, Rosa Smith, Oprah Winfrey, Nelson Mandela, Richard Branson, and Bono came from meager beginnings, and through risk and decision-making created a road to success. All of them have had a profound effect on the world community—they all dreamed dreams of a better future and passionately pursued their visions in spite of any opposition to them.

I believe that this ability to take action and bring dreams into a physical reality changes the world. Again, each of us has the same opportunity every day.

Wright

Well, I appreciate your even mentioning my name.

Bishop

I wouldn't be in this book if you hadn't given me the opportunity.

Wright

Have people influenced your journey and how have they contributed?

Bishop

I have genuinely been influenced by many mentors. The people who have been there at turning points in my life provided tried and proven ways to reach their goals—ways that I've emulated. My mentors have been men and women who have demanded excellence in their lives. They saw my potential and they had vision, compassion, patience, and generosity of spirit that contributed to my development. These mentors and teachers appeared at critical turning points in my life. They helped me develop self-regard and self-trust. I'll forever be thankful to each of them.

My clients and friends have also given me the privilege of their trust, faith, and perseverance as I walk with them daily on their journeys. They have been an inspiration and have allowed me to witness their greatness and achievements.

I recently read a quote by Steven Stern in an article in *The Financial Times*. He remarked on a recent study that attempted to define the elements of a great leader. I think his quote sums up my interview today. He said, "Leadership, it turns out, is a team sport." The people who have influenced me contributed to my leadership ability and success. We are all part of a team and are interdependent upon each other for our successful accomplishments. We never walk the road to success alone.

Wright

Looking back, would you say that your life has taken you in the direction that you intended?

Bishop

Looking back I have used many road maps to get me where I wanted to go. Each of those road maps helped me reinvent myself when necessary or redirected my course to get me to my destination. Each experience has given me a better understanding of myself and what it is to be a human being. It's clear to me that I will explore many more roads as I move forward.

Wright

Well, it seems to me that you're traveling in the right direction. I really appreciate all the time you've taken today to discuss this important subject of building one's road map to success.

Bishop

David, thank you so much. I always enjoy talking with you.

Wright

Today we've been talking with Jo Anne Bishop, PhD. She is the CEO of Crossing Bridges and Associates, which is a coaching, consulting, and conflict mediation company. Luckily, she lives in one of the most beautiful places on earth—Honolulu, Hawaii. She has co-authored *Success Strategies: The High Achiever's Guide to Success* and *Success is a State of Mind.* I think she knows a lot about success.

Thank you so much, Dr. Bishop, for being with us today on *Roadmap to Success.*

Bishop

Thank you, David.

ABOUT DR. JO ANNE BISHOP

Dr. Jo Anne Bishop is founder and CEO of Crossing Bridges & Associates. She is a Certified Professional Coach with a national and international client base. A top performer and leader in her field, she brings twenty years of expertise to coaching, communications, organizational psychology, and training development. She completed a highly successful psychotherapy and consulting practice in Beverly Hills and Long Beach, California, to create Crossing Bridges & Associates. A gifted speaker, author, presenter, and coach, she has developed dynamic, experientially based programs that propel clients to the leading edge in the competitive marketplace. Her programs integrate goal-setting, strategic decision-making, and accountability with the power of the intuitive/creative mind. Her credentials include graduate degrees in Counseling Psychology, Public Policy, and Administration. She holds certifications in education and clinical hypnotherapy and co-authored *Success Strategies: The High Achiever's Guide to Success* and *Success is a State of Mind*. Dr. Bishop's professional memberships include: The American Association of Family Therapists, the American Association of Psychotherapy and Medical Hypnosis, the International Coach Federation, International Coach Association, American Society of Training and Development, the International Speakers Network, and the Hawaii Speakers Network. She and her husband reside in the beautiful Hawaiian Islands.

Jo Anne Bishop, PhD, MPA
Crossing Bridges & Associates
6800 Kalanianaole Highway, #126
Honolulu, Hawaii 96825
562.760.3009 (Cell)
808.772.0266 (Office)
crossingbridges@hawaii.rr.com
www.execandbusinesscoach.com

ROADMAP to SUCCESS 15

An interview with ...

TED BRASSFIELD

David Wright (Wright)

Today we're talking with Ted Brassfield. Ted Brassfield is a successful author, speaker, and workshop facilitator. His book, *The Law of Attraction Workbook—The Seven Step Process for Creating a Passionate and Purposeful Life,* is a practical application for using The Law of Attraction in creating a successful, passionate, and balanced life.

Ted is a Life Coach, accredited by the International Coaching Federation and specializes in supporting clients and workshop participants in creating a passionate, balanced life that is fulfilled, powerful, and successful. Ted also has a specialized niche in coaching clients in writing their first book. He supports them in picking topics, overcoming writer's block, and expressing passion through their writing.

Ted takes his corporate and individual clients through a step-by-step process of creating a vision and living it in all aspects of their lives from career success, living healthy, finding passion and purpose, and creating relationships that are filled with intimacy and enjoyment.

Ted is a graduate of Michigan State University with a BS degree in Electrical Engineering. He has had more than twenty years with corporate America, managing multimillion-dollar projects and supervising hundreds of employees. He left corporate

America to pursue his passion of making a difference and changing lives through volunteering, coaching, and writing.

Ted, welcome to *Roadmap to Success*.

How do you define success, Ted?

Ted Brassfield (Brassfield)

I would define success as realizing our potential in all aspects of life—financially, spiritually, emotionally, intellectually, as well as in areas of health, relationships, and of course, finding, living, and enjoying our passions. We are all unique. The meaning of success is different from person to person. We are all connected because, when we realize our potential, we not only attain personal and professional success, we serve and contribute to those we touch directly in our lives, and beyond that, to the community, the planet, and generations to come. Once we understand that financial and material goal attainment is not fulfilling in itself, and that true fulfillment is going beyond the material, we are truly on the road to success.

Wright

What do you think are the biggest obstacles people face in trying to become successful?

Brassfield

It is actually a perfect time to ask that question this early in our dialogue. The reason is because as soon as we try to step out and create something new in our lives, like a goal or vision for our lives, immediately a "Second Force" of equal and opposite magnitude comes to meet the first force of energy, enthusiasm, and passion of our new idea, goal, or vision. The name for this force is "The Law of Opposites."

Think back in your own life when you've tried or wanted to do something new. All of a sudden, all the reasons why it can't be done come charging into your head and heart like the cavalry. The way to handle this is to know that it is all part of the process—it is all part of the human condition—and to understand that when you feel it, embrace it with a knowing nod, and say to yourself, "Ah, I am on the right track."

Usually we quit or change course as soon as this Second Force hits us, and our dreams are squashed. We go back to living much smaller lives than we could be living.

We are unfulfilled and embracing the excuses that we have created for not achieving the success we are designed to have.

The following obstacles are actually how the Second Force/Law of Opposites shows up in us to block or not allow the achievement of our success:

Self-limiting Beliefs: These are beliefs that began at an early age in our childhood. We interpreted these events to mean "something was wrong with *me.*" We then went on to gather evidence or proof that this was true, and for our entire lives we see the world through the filter of these limiting beliefs.

Here is an example of how this occurs: A child asks his father to take him fishing after he gets home from work. The father agrees to take him fishing that evening. The child waits all day with the anticipation of spending time with his father. In fact, the child is fantasizing all day with anticipation of catching a large fish and impressing his dad. The father gets tied up at work and forgets about the promise he made to his son and comes home too late to take him fishing. Even though the father apologizes, the child interprets this event in the wrong way—that his father doesn't love him because if he did, he would not have forgotten about him. A wound is created. The child looks at the world through the filter of not being lovable and gathers evidence from then on to prove he isn't lovable. He sabotages relationships with people who try to love him and he picks women who will recreate additional situations for unlovable interpretations to occur.

These Self-limiting Beliefs, or Shadow Beliefs, are very powerful and can control our lives because they operate in the subconscious. We don't know that they are the main reasons why we are unsuccessful in achieving what we desire. Fortunately there are ways to overcome them so they don't control our lives.

Debbie Ford does fantastic work with understanding Shadow Beliefs and even using these beliefs to support us in attaining even more success, wholeness, and fulfillment than we would have had without them because they are part of our unique recipe that makes us who we are. As with the child who believed he was unlovable based on his interpretation of his father coming home late from work, if he could embrace his unlovable shadow, he could use it to support other adults and children who have the same wound he has. He could use his experience in a powerful way by going into a field such as psychology and have a successful career teaching, writing, and speaking on this subject. He would be, after all, an expert on this subject, thanks to his unlovable Shadow Belief!

Not enough "x:" A secondary level of limiting beliefs is that we do not have enough time, resources, and money to be successful. When these thoughts and fears hit our psyche, it feels as though all of the passion and excitement of our dreams are dashed. It is as though someone stuck a pin in our success balloon and the air of possibility is being deflated. This is the time to have faith in our dreams and not faith in our fears. This is the time to know that what feels like a true reality of limited resources is only a belief. It's FEAR: **F**alse **E**vidence **A**ppearing **R**eal. The true reality is that we can create a new reality through refocusing on our desires and not focusing on the false evidence.

At this stage, it is important to know that you have the power to create a new reality in every area of your life. The necessary step is to realize that you do not have to know *how* to attain the time, resources, or money. Once you are focused on your desires with positive energy and emotion (passion, enthusiasm), you will be in alignment with your desires, and The Law of Attraction will respond with all the tools you need to be successful in every aspect of your life that you are in alignment with.

Lack of support: When we try to accomplish our goals, achieve our vision, and be successful in any aspect of our lives, having support in terms of positive people, groups, and institutions/organizations is critical. Surround yourself with people who are committed to listening to your vision and goals without "constructive criticism." Create an agreement with people you designate as supporters that they will only feed back positive responses and be cheerleaders for you and your vision. Agree to be a cheerleader for them in accomplishing their goals and vision as well.

The basis of the cheerleading agreement is that you both have trust that your partner has the answers within them to know what to do and how to do it. The cheerleader's role is to only provide emotional support, to keep the enthusiasm high, and feel our passion with us. If you need expertise in an area, then hire a consultant. If you need help in visioning and goal setting, hire a coach. If you need emotional support at a deep level, then hire a therapist. But for support in keeping the passion alive for your vision, then designate cheerleaders. They have a major impact in supporting you in achieving success and they are free!

Focusing on "what is:" This means focusing on our current circumstances as opposed to what our desires are. As an example: You are not happy with your current circumstances in relationships, health, or financial issues. You find yourself focusing on them, complaining about them, and being resentful and angry. This focus attracts more of what you do not want. You will then have more to complain about, which results in more focus on what you do not want. I call this the *"Circle of Stuckness."* We start with our present situation, we focus on it with negative energy by complaining, beating ourselves up for even being in this circumstance, or we blame others for it. We attract more of the same, and then start the process all over again. The Law of Attraction is working to fulfill what we are focusing on so we get more of what we don't want because of the negative focus.

In order to move out of our *Circle of Stuckness*, we must refocus on our vision, dreams, passions, and desires, and embrace our current circumstance. This will result in attracting new circumstances that are in alignment with our vision. We must remember that we brought about our current circumstances through our previous thoughts, energy, and focus via The Law of Attraction and we can create new results or circumstances by refocusing on what we want, not what we do not want.

One technique I use with my coaching clients is to find gifts, insights, awareness, and benefits in the current situation that they are not happy with. As an example:

Current Situation (What is): Client doesn't currently have a soul mate and wants to be happily married. She cannot seem to attract her soul mate no matter how much she wants, prays, and hopes for one.

Response: This continuous focus on *not* having a soul mate results in The Law of Attraction creating more circumstances whereby she is unable to find her soul mate. The Law of Attraction responds to the energy and focus of what she is offering. Since she is offering to the universe negative energy and focus on the lack of a soul mate, the response is more lack. It would be contrary to The Law of Attraction to respond with the circumstances that would create this soul mate in her life because her attention is on *not* having a soul mate currently.

Action Steps:
- Refocus energy and attention from what is (lack of a soul mate) to knowing that her soul mate is out there with the circumstances being created right now to bring him forth into her life.

211

- Look at all the qualities and attributes she wants in a soul mate and be them herself. If she wants him to be trustworthy and if she wants spirituality in her soul mate, she must have those qualities in herself before she will attract it.

When she finds herself focusing on what is—her lack of having a soul mate—then look for the positive aspects of not having a soul mate right now. This will dissipate the negative energy and focus from lack to allowing an easy flow of energy to her desire.

Examples of positive gifts or benefits of not having a soul mate:

- She can work on personal, emotional, professional, and financial issues.
- She can de-clutter her house, office, and car.
- She can enjoy her time alone and pamper herself doing things she loves.
- She can travel with friends.
- She can take classes for fun and enjoyment.
- She can reconnect with friends and family on a deeper level.

By focusing on the positive aspects of her current situation as opposed to the lack, she can embrace and love her life as it is now and be available to attract her desired soul mate.

Lack of Forgiveness: When we feel victimized, angry, resentful, and envious toward other people or ourselves, it results in negative energy being offered out into the universe. This blocks or slows down positive energy flow toward our desires, preventing them from being manifested. Do forgiveness work. Realize that The Law of Attraction is monitoring energy (emotion). If you are offering out to the universe negative energy, you won't get back positive results. A successful life cannot be created in the midst of negative unforgiving energy.

Wright

What makes your perspective unique?

Brassfield

I specialize in Law of Attraction Coaching. As you know, in recent years much has been written about The Law of Attraction and to many people it seems like hocus-pocus or poppycock for the lack of stronger words.

What I bring is a practical application of The Law of Attraction so that clients, readers, and participants in my workshops can use this powerful law as a road map to their success. I have found that unless you provide an easy-to-follow, step-by-step pathway on how to use The Law of Attraction, it is just another flavor of the month concept that will sit gathering dust on our bookshelves or just thought of as a theoretical concept that's nice to know, but impossible to use effectively. My book, *The Law of Attraction Workbook—The Seven-Step Process for Creating a Passionate and Purposeful Life,* goes into details that I will briefly highlight in this book as well as add new concepts not covered in my book.

Wright

Your speaking, coaching, and book are focused on The Law of Attraction. Will you describe it in a simple way?

Brassfield

The Law of Attraction says:

- Like attracts like.
- We create our own reality by our frequency and intensity of what we focus on.
- Positive energy and focus creates and attracts positive results.
- Negative energy and focus creates negative results.

Focus is defined as directed thoughts, words, and actions. I use energy, emotions, and vibrations synonymously. When we focus on our desires with positive emotions (excitement, enthusiasm, passion), we are offering vibrations out into the universe, and The Law of Attraction responds by matching and multiplying the energy and providing positive results. It responds with even more than you asked for because we live in an abundant universe—the results are even greater than we have asked for. When we focus on our desires with negative emotions (fear, hopelessness, anger) or focus on our current circumstances in a negative way, we are requesting more negativity in our lives and The Law of Attraction responds with negative results.

Wright

How can we use The Law of Attraction to attain success?

Brassfield

I will provide two pathways to use The Law of Attraction to attain success. The first method I will call the neutral or non-spiritual application of The Law of Attraction. The second method is a more spiritual application of it.

Non-Spiritual Application of The Law of Attraction to attain success:

The first step is merely to define your vision and goals. What do you want to attain in your life to be successful as you define it? What is your big vision for your life in every area?

This is a major first step, so spend lots of time. Employ a coach or whatever is needed to get clear about what your vision of success is for you. From there we go to goals and timelines that are in alignment with your vision.

The next step is distinctive to Law of Attraction Coaching versus other more traditional coaching methodologies. Instead of jumping right into action steps once goals are defined, focus on the vision, with strong positive emotions of enthusiasm, excitement, and passion and continue this until the next steps (action steps) come to you from the response you receive from the universe.

Focusing on our vision means we are fantasizing, imagining, and in wonderment of how the successful accomplishment of the vision would impact our lives and those around us. The focus is on the vision as if it is already manifested, not on how to achieve it by focusing on problem solving, figuring out the next steps, and analyzing the so-called roadblocks.

The next steps will come to you as a response from the universe, not from your left-brain, logical conscious mind. These steps come in the form of new ideas, action steps, conversations you need to have, and circumstances that are created to move you toward the manifestation of your vision.

So in summary:

1.) Create your vision of success. Define it in all aspects of your life.
2.) Focus with positive energy on your vision.

3.) Let the action steps—the road map to successful achievement of your vision—come *from* your focus, meditation, and visualizations.

4.) The Law of Attraction will bring the circumstances into effect to achieve your vision.

5.) Continuously adjust your action steps, and even adjust your vision and goals as new ideas flow to you from the universe (Continuous Improvement).

Wright

How does God fit into using The Law of Attraction to help me attain success if I am a spiritual/religious person?

Brassfield

It is actually more effective to use The Law of Attraction in a spiritual context than not because you can partner with God to co-create a successful, abundant life. Faith adds power, belief, energy, and hope. Partnering with God and co-creating with Him can make the difference in overcoming the blocks that traditionally hold us back and keep us smaller than our potential. The spiritual application of The Law of Attraction takes us much deeper and creates results at even higher levels of fulfillment because the vision of success is much larger than financial and material goals. By incorporating a God consciousness, we are starting from a sacred space of abundance, love, power, forgiveness, gratitude, wholeness, and passion. When we start from our own conscious mind, without incorporating a higher power, we are limited by our wounds, self-limiting beliefs, and ego.

The Law of Attraction still works without consciously incorporating God, but the obstacles are much more present and powerful and harder to move past.

So let's start with creating that vision of success, co-creating it with God. In this space, everyone and everything is connected, interwoven spiritually through God. The spiritual you is where your true vision of success will originate. This sacred place within you holds the key to passion, fulfillment, and success. It is unencumbered by the wounded ego or conscious mind that limits your possibilities and potential. This is the place where abundance is the reality and there is no lack or limit to your vision.

This true vision comes from the divine spark within us, so we must be connected to our source in order to truly hear what God desires for us. How do we make this connection? This is done through deep breathing, meditation, and prayer. In this space of connectedness you will feel love, gratitude, and forgiveness flowing through you.

Remember and remind yourself how satisfying it feels to be in this euphoric state and reconnect with these feelings throughout the day. With practice, you can achieve this state of euphoria, no matter what the situation or circumstances are, by being in the present and connecting with the God spirit within you.

From this space, ask this question: God, what is your true vision for me?

The answers will come in the form of thoughts, dreams, ideas, situations, circumstances, and conversations that stimulate and excite you. Keep a journal. Watch for signs that are in alignment. Listen for words. Notice thoughts and see and feel the responses from this God space.

Your true vision (that which is in alignment with God) will be clear to you if you continue mediation and prayer and focus on that question.

Now that you have the true vision for yourself (your soul's vision), you surrender to knowing that you do not have the answers of *how* to achieve this vision successfully from your conscious, logical, action-orientated mind. You must have faith that your vision will be attained and that the answers of *how* to manifest your vision will come from the same source where your true vision came from. This means continue your prayer and meditation even after you have your true vision, and listen for the *how* and the action steps that will flow to you. You will notice that circumstances are being created to support you in achieving your vision, some that you may have never thought even possible. This is The Law of Attraction responding!

A note about prayer: prayer works! We just must understand that when we pray, we are making a request to God to fulfill our desires. If we pray with positive energy and emotion, and a faith or belief that God will answer our prayers, then they will be fulfilled.

The mechanism called The Law of Attraction process that responds to our prayers and desires is God's response. If we pray with negative emotion, fear, anxiety, disbelief, and hopelessness, then God answers these prayers too, even though the answers to our prayers won't look like what we thought we were requesting. The answers to these fear-based prayers will look to us like the opposite of what we are asking for. The good news is that there is learning and opportunity in every circumstance, and as long as we do not stay focused on the circumstances with negative energy, we can always reset and use The Law of Attraction to create new circumstances more in alignment with what we desire. By co-creating our prayers/desires with God we are proactively and deliberately co-creating the successful life we desire.

Summary:

1.) Use meditation, prayer, and breathing to get connected with God.

2.) Ask God, "What is your true vision for me?"

3.) Let the action steps come from your continuing meditation, prayer, and breathing for the attainment of how to successfully achieve your true vision.

4.) The Law of Attraction will bring the circumstances, people, and events to achieve your true vision.

5.) Continuously adjust your action steps, vision, and goals as new ideas flow to you from your connection with God.

Wright

Will you tell our readers a little about what drives you to be successful?

Brassfield

I let my passions drive me. I am committed to living a passionate life. This does not translate into a self-indulgent, narcissistic existence. It results in loving my life and supporting others in loving their lives as well. I want to see people reach their potential and be happy. I want them to live their passions, have love, self-awareness, and success in their lives. I have a true passion for it.

When I consciously discovered that my passion was to serve others in a way that supports them in living their passions, fulfillment, and success, I was driven to find an avenue to serve more than my friends and family—I wanted to serve in a bigger way.

Before I consciously discovered The Law of Attraction, it was working to create a way for me to serve my passion at a high level. It created the circumstances that would bring coaching into my awareness. I found a way to live my passions in a real way and be trained to do it at professional level. As I focused positively and enthusiastically on my passions, larger responses from the universe started flowing to me to give me opportunities to play at a higher level and impact more people through speaking, teaching workshops, and writing books.

I am driven to support others in living as passionately, abundantly, and successfully as they desire and I don't let excuses, circumstances, or any dream-stoppers get in my way.

Wright

What is the message you want people to hear so that they can learn from your success?

Brassfield

Find what excites you and live it, love it, enjoy it, feel it, and taste it. Start with what you enjoy now and practice a higher level of enjoyment than you ever have before. Start with simple things that you enjoy such as your favorite snack, favorite song, or favorite movie. Taste the snack, listen to the song, or see the movie as though it was your first time. Slow down, be in the present moment, and commit to your own enjoyment of these simple things. Expand it to more and more situations, activities, and even conversations. Enjoy these precious moments. What you are doing is practicing being passionate. The more you practice, the more you bring about more things to be passionate about.

As you become more connected to the things you love in your life, the more you will want others to experience enjoyment in their lives. Love your life regardless of your circumstances. Love your life *and* create new circumstances that will allow you to attract more of what you desire to be successful, fulfilled, and abundant.

Wright

How do you balance your success in your life?

Brassfield

I take time for myself. The masculine in me meditates, breathes, and enjoys the stillness and nothingness that is peaceful to me. The feminine in me listens to music, dances, writes, and enjoys being pampered. I also balance my success with other things I enjoy such as tennis, nature, friends, and family.

I am committed to creating and maintaining high quality relationships and letting go of toxic ones. I am committed to my own personal growth and spend time reading books, going to workshops, and in therapy/coaching for my own awareness, insights, and fulfillment. I go to church so I can also grow spiritually.

Wright

Who are the people who have served as your role models for success?

Brassfield

It is impossible to list all of them. I hesitate because I am concerned about leaving out important influences in my life. My personal belief is that I have learned something from everyone. Here is a short list and a note about why they are my role models:

- Lucille and Theodore Brassfield: for instilling love, values, and caring for others in me.
- Marianne Williamson: who introduced me to spirituality on a broader and deeper level.
- Debbie Ford: for giving me an avenue to express my passion.
- Cheryl Richardson: who challenged me to live my passion and be unstoppable.
- Dave Ellis: for his coaching methodology and vision.
- Rev Jim Lee: for his mentoring and friendship.
- David Deida: for his work with sexuality and spirituality.
- Sandy Parker: for her therapeutic work in self-awareness.
- Renaissance Unity: the congregants, staff, ministers, and choir who support and inspire me to continue my spiritual growth to love and serve God.

Wright

Are there additional tools that you can share with us?

Brassfield

The *Circle of Stuckness* basically illustrates how we get stuck in focusing on our current circumstances. Since The Law of Attraction brings about more of what we focus on, we attract more of the circumstances we do not want and are stuck in a circle that does not serve us. It is a vicious circle that does not allow us to manifest our desires. We concentrate our energies, conversations, and focus on "what is" and not what we want, so we just bring about more of the same. The way to move beyond this circle is to focus outside the circle on what we desire with positive energy.

On my Web site you can order the "Steps for the Road Map to Success" using The Law of Attraction. It is an illustration of the steps needed to manifest your vision and goals using The Law of Attraction. It is a powerful yet simple tool to better understand how to move from the *Circle of Stuckness* to the steps to the manifestation of your desires.

Wright

Any concluding remarks?

We all have the power to create success in our lives. No matter what our current circumstances are, no matter what your age, gender, race, physical or financial situation, we live in an abundant universe and we can achieve our desires and be successful in all areas of our lives. We need to believe in ourselves, be focused on our desires, find and live our passions, love life, contribute to the world, forgive ourselves and others, and have gratitude for every circumstance and experience, no matter how good or bad we think it is.

ABOUT TED BRASSFIELD

Ted Brassfield is a successful author, speaker, and workshop facilitator. His book, The Law of Attraction Workbook—The Seven Step Process for Creating a Passionate and Purposeful Life, is a practical application for using The Law of Attraction in creating a successful, passionate, balanced life.

Ted is a Life Coach, accredited by the International Coaching Federation, and he specializes in supporting clients and workshop participants in creating a passionate, balanced life that is fulfilled, powerful, and successful. Ted graduated from the Debbie Ford Integrative Coaching Program in 2002 and has been a Life Coach for six years.

Ted takes his corporate and individual clients through a step-by-step process of creating a vision and living it, in all aspects of their lives from career success to living healthy, finding passion and purpose, and creating relationships that are filled with intimacy and enjoyment.

Ted also specializes in supporting clients in writing their first book. He helps them pick topics, overcoming writer's block, and expressing themselves with passion through their writing.

Ted brings a passionate energy to his workshops that incorporates interactive exercises, real-life examples, and successful strategies to his programs. He creates enthusiasm, fun, and energy so that participants' goals, purpose, and mission are clarified, created, and implemented. A pathway to happiness, passion, and excitement about creating a positive change in the lives of participants and those they touch is provided in easy to understand, but powerful workshops, seminars, and one-on-one coaching relationships.

Ted is a graduate of Michigan State University with a BS degree in Electrical Engineering. He has had more than twenty years with corporate America, managing multimillion-dollar projects and supervising hundreds of employees. He left corporate America to pursue his passion of making a difference and changing lives through volunteering, coaching, and writing.

Ted Brassfield
ted@pathwaytopotential.com
ted@bookwriting-coach.com
pathwaytopotential.com
bookwriting-coach.com